FINANCIAL
SERIAL KILLERS

FINANCIAL
SERIAL KILLERS

Inside the World of Wall Street
Money Hustlers, Swindlers, and Con Men

TOM AJAMIE AND BRUCE KELLY

A Herman Graf Book
Skyhorse Publishing

Skyhorse Publishing books may be purchased in bulk at special discounts for sales promotion, corporate gifts, fund-raising, or educational purposes. Special editions can also be created to specifications. For details, contact the Special Sales Department, Skyhorse Publishing, 555 Eighth Avenue, Suite 903, New York, NY 10018 or info@skyhorsepublishing.com.

www.skyhorsepublishing.com

10 9 8 7 6 5 4 3 2 1

Library of Congress Cataloging-in-Publication Data

Ajamie, Tom.
  Financial serial killers : inside the world of wall street money hustlers, swindlers, and con men / Tom Ajamie & Bruce Kelly.
    p. cm.
  ISBN 978-1-61608-031-0
  1. Fraud--United States. 2. Swindlers and swindling--United States. 3. Investments--United States. I. Kelly, Bruce. II. Title.
  HV6695.A35 2010
  362.88--dc22

                                        2010000144
Printed in the United States of America

"Radix malorum est cupiditas."

Greed is the root of all evil.

—"The Pardoner's Tale," Chaucer

"Rule number one: Never lose money.

Rule number two: Never forget rule number one."

—Warren Buffett

Contents

FINANCIAL
SERIAL KILLERS

CHAPTER
ONE

Financial
Serial Killers

Sadly, Bernie Madoff is no different than hundreds, if not thousands, of common thieves that today blight the American landscape and put you and your life savings in danger.

Yes, he stole and shifted around billions of dollars, perpetuating most likely the greatest fraud in American history. However, if one looks at his manner and methods, at how he actually did it, the conclusion is clear. Simply put, fraudsters like Bernie Madoff—we call them financial serial killers—won't be found only on Wall Street. In fact, they operate in towns large and small across the United States.

The seduction techniques used by Bernie Madoff to attract investors are the same well-worn tricks used over and over by financial schemers across the country. The financial con man always paints a picture of himself as someone who has a great deal of financial knowledge (certainly more than his victim) and a "proven" track record of having made a lot of money for others. He'll likely show some piece of paper acknowledging his outsized investment gains. He'll tell a tale of having spun riches for others. He'll convince you of how he alone has, through his hard work, devised a "can't fail" means of making money: be it some type of overlooked investment product, some type of hedging technique, or inside knowledge possessed by only him or his investment team.

Personal relations are imperative to the success of the financial con man. He is a master at building them. He will bond with his victim, emphasizing their common interests. Did you both attend the same high school or college? Do you share the same religion or ethnic background? Did you, perhaps, belong to the same club or have kids at the same school? Or, by coincidence, did you both grow up in the same neighborhood?

Maybe, if the con man is particularly lucky, you even know some of the same people. That is particularly wonderful, because people seem to believe that, if you and I know the same people then, well, we must share the same values and we can now trust one another. So what the financial serial killer eventually achieves is to cause you, the victim, to believe in him. To trust. To feel comfortable. To let down your guard. All this is done with such skill that even the smartest among us fails to do the most basic research into the man we will entrust to hold our life savings, our children's college money, and the money we will use to buy our food and our medicine when we near the end of our life and are too old to work.

It would be ridiculous for us to make blanket statements about a firm or an industry. This book is not saying that all stockbrokers lack ethics or are somehow evil. Our goal is to help investors separate the wheat from the chaff to help identify a broker or adviser who does have questionable business practices so you can find a good one.

In fact, there are hundreds—and perhaps even thousands—of such financial serial killers lurking in the financial landscape right now. One group of securities regulators—FINRA—recently estimated there are fifteen thousand ex-stockbrokers barred from the industry. Until late 2009, information about brokers, even those who have been banned from selling securities because of criminal and outrageous behavior, was removed from public viewing after they had been out of the securities business for two years. This was the norm even though FINRA encouraged investors to use public Web sites to check out brokers. The federal government had the good sense to address the issue, and the records of such bad brokers are now permanently public. However, many brokers banned from the securities business have surfaced in the spate of recent frauds and Ponzi schemes that have cost investors billions of dollars.

The FBI and Congress have finally taken notice. The 2008 stock market collapse exposed so many schemes that the FBI in 2009 began a new investment fraud investigation for every day of the year.

"High yield investment fraud schemes have many variations, all of which are characterized by offers of low risk investments, guaranteeing an unusually high rate of return," testified Kevin Perkins, assistant director of the FBI, before the Senate Judiciary Committee in December 2009. He explained that the crimes weren't complicated. "Victims are enticed by the prospect of easy money and a fast turnaround."

The financial serial killer's ability to make investors hand over their money is a key to fueling such frauds, Perkins noted: "The most common form of these frauds is the Ponzi scheme, which is named after early twentieth-century criminal Charles Ponzi.

These schemes use money collected from new victims, rather than profits from an underlying business venture, to pay the high rates of return promised to earlier investors. This arrangement gives investors the impression there is a legitimate, money-making enterprise behind the fraudster's story; but in reality, unwitting investors are the only source of funding."

"As the financial crisis expanded, drying up investment funds and causing investors to begin seeking returns of their principal, investment fraud schemes began to unravel." The number of investment frauds was staggering, Perkins told Congress. In the fiscal year 2009, the FBI saw a 105 percent increase in new high-yield investment fraud investigations when compared to 2008 (314 versus 154, and many had losses exceeding $100 million). "Many of the Ponzi scheme investigations have an international nexus and have affected thousands of victims," Perkins said.

Yes, 2009 was indeed a rough year for Ponzi schemers. The recession unraveled nearly four times as many of the investment scams as fell apart in 2008, with "Ponzi" becoming a buzzword again thanks to the collapse of Madoff's $50 billion plot.

Tens of thousands of investors, some of them losing their life savings, watched more than $16.5 billion disappear like smoke in 2009, according to an Associated Press analysis of scams in all fifty states.

While the dollar figure was lower than in 2008, that's only because Madoff—who pleaded guilty in 2009 and is serving a 150-year prison sentence—was arrested in December 2008 and didn't count toward 2009's total.

While enforcement efforts have ramped up in large part because of the discovery of Madoff's fraud, the main reason so many Ponzi schemes have come to light is clear.

"The financial meltdown has resulted in the exposure of numerous fraudulent schemes that otherwise might have gone undetected for a longer period of time," said Lanny Breuer, assistant attorney general for the U.S. Justice Department's criminal division, in an interview with the Associated Press.

The financial serial killers pose as financial whizzes, sell investors bogus or unnecessary products that they claim are safe, or simply gin up investment returns. Like Madoff, the financial serial killer lives a swell life on stolen money.

Investors are routinely left with their life savings wiped out and no way to get it back.

Financial serial killers are smart.

They exude confidence and credibility.

They speak with self-assurance, hold themselves confidently, and seem to know their stuff. They are believable. Their credibility is often enhanced by their references. Getting the first "sucker" is the most difficult task, but once they have a respectable chump in their pack, it's easier to get the others.

They are often seen as "pillars of the community."

They are charming.

They have the aura of success. A plush office, expensive home, and nice car are essential.

Like Madoff, regarded by many industry veterans as a "broker's broker," financial serial killers operate and pose under any number of familiar guises. They have familiar or trust-invoking titles such as insurance agent or financial consultant. They sell themselves as the investor's trusted financial adviser. Unlike Madoff, financial serial killers usually steal tens or hundreds of millions rather than billions of dollars. But the toll on or damage to a life cannot be counted in coin.

According to the FBI in 2009, American investors were getting ripped off at a prodigious rate, often by people they consider dear, true friends or advisers. These dear "true friends" include investment advisers who kneel and pray with their clients, mortgage brokers who promise financial salvation with a fancy yet fake new product, and businessmen who seemingly rain money on their clients.

Madoff's scam should come as no surprise. Before Madoff confessed his crimes to his sons in December 2008, stories of financial serial killers who robbed investors of their life savings seemed more prevalent than ever. Even members of law enforcement were not immune to the scamsters' charms.

One recent victim of investment fraud was the police chief of Birdsboro, Pennsylvania, a town of about 5,000 citizens, where kids attend the public schools of the Daniel Boone School District. The chief, Theodore R. Roth, was one of 800 clients whose local mortgage broker had bamboozled clients into taking out loans for sums greater than they needed to borrow. The broker, Wesley A. Snyder, promised to invest that extra cash and pay off their mortgages through a complex proprietary system that no one but he could understand—just like Madoff.

In the end, Snyder's promise was a sham, and his clients lost more than $29 million. Snyder couldn't put an end to the pain as he lost control of his plan. In fact, he made it worse. As the system failed, he, like Madoff, wound up creating a Ponzi scheme, using money from new investors to pay off the loans of other clients. "I feel like a schmuck," the local police chief Roth said in September 2007, days after the collapse of Snyder's companies. "All these years in law enforcement, and I fall victim to this." (In certain instances in this book, the names of the players have been changed, but the stories are accurate and true.)

Looking for a safe haven in times of economic turmoil, investors may be more prone than ever to trust in potential scams. It could be giving money to a member of their church who promises fabulous guaranteed returns or finally taking the plunge and investing with their best friend's stock guru who claims to have a foolproof way of making money.

Such beliefs could lead you into the hands of a financial serial killer. Such investment thieves proliferate in dark times, when some investors become more desperate than ever to increase their money.

The danger to investors from financial serial killers won't disappear anytime soon.

Human gullibility is a burgeoning area of psychological research.

"There are few areas where skepticism is more important than how one invests one's life savings," wrote Stephen Greenspan, a psychologist, in the *Wall Street Journal*. "Yet intelligent and educated people, some of them naïve about finance and others quite knowledgeable, have been ruined by schemes that turned out to be highly dubious and quite often fraudulent."

Greenspan should know. He invested with Bernie Madoff.

CHAPTER
TWO

The Little Old Lady Who Invested with Buffett and Was Fleeced by Insurance Agents

After more than sixty years of a happy and stable marriage, Lillian Wentz lost her husband, Luke, in 1997. This sad change came with an incredible burden. At the age of eighty-nine, Lillian was suddenly responsible for a treasure that she and her husband had owned for more than fifty years: Berkshire Hathaway stock that was worth $24 million.

This is a story about financial serial killers sniffing out a family's money and then disguising a scam as a financial transaction that appeared legtimate to its victims.

Like many women of her generation who have lost their husbands, Lillian for the first time ever was in charge of the family finances. These new responsibilities ranged from simple tasks such as balancing a checkbook and paying the bills to the burden of safely guarding—and passing along—the family fortune. That's a staggering responsibility for a woman who came of age during the Great Depression.

This burden must have weighed heavily on Lillian's mind. The fact that she was as rich as a duchess would very likely have been a shock to her. Lillian and Luke were the offspring of pioneers.

Luke was born in Independence, Oklahoma, in 1907, and Lillian was born in Essex, Iowa, the same year.

They worked hard their entire lives. After graduating from college in 1929—the eve of the Great Depression—Lillian returned home to work with her family picking cotton in the fields. She then landed a teaching job by chance: two teachers who had been hired by the local school were in a car accident and resigned. Lillian was offered the job. As a young schoolteacher she earned $100 per month and worked in a two-story red brick schoolhouse. When it rained, she rode the family horse, Lulu, to the school house to work.

Despite their increasing wealth, Lillian and Luke never lived it up, but continued working the family farm where they settled early in their marriage. Luke's dedication to the family business was acknowledged by his farming peers, and as he neared retirement he was honored as "Cotton Farmer of the Year."

By a stroke of good fortune they had grown to be wealthy. The Berkshire stock had been bought in 1946, when the company didn't even exist but its forerunner did: Lillian and her husband Luke had paid $6,600 for 500 shares of the Hathaway Manufacturing Co., a textile company based in New Bedford, Massachusetts.

In an age when families typically carry thousands of dollars of credit card debt, the balance sheet of Lillian's assets and liabilities after Luke's death is almost beyond belief. She was about as far in the black as any individual could be. She owed nothing on her home or car, and she never applied for a credit card. Her investment assets and personal assets had grown to more than $27 million. The eighty-nine-year-old Lillian was set to live comfortably, with absolutely no financial worries for the rest of her days.

Yet, despite her incredible wealth—or perhaps because of it—Lillian was vulnerable. It would prove impossible for her to guard the family treasure alone. This is where family dynamics can cause people like Lillian to be vulnerable to attacks by financial con artists. Lillian's son, Luke Jr., his wife, and their three sons respected her privacy. They believed they had no right to interfere with her business decisions, including that mountain of Berkshire Hathaway stock.

In the months after her husband Luke's death, Lillian began having difficulties. She was showing signs of senile dementia. She was losing track of things; she began storing her mail in the dishwasher. Her immediate family, out of respect, weren't about to stick their noses into her business—even when it came to her savings.

Many older women who lose their husbands or partners are overwhelmed by the responsibilities they must face alone for the first time, including the responsibility of the family's wealth or estate, large or small. It's only natural to turn to members of the extended family or community to help carry that load. Lillian, after her husband's death, looked for that help. She turned to a distant cousin, who was a lawyer near the small Texas town where she and Luke had lived for over sixty years.

Lillian wanted Cousin Bill to answer a simple question: what was the best way to protect and preserve this family fortune so she could hand that stock over some day to her son, his wife, and her three grandsons?

• --

This is a simple but extremely important lesson for investors to learn. They often fall prey to scams at a vulnerable point in their lives. So investors must be vigilant and watchful at times of grief or personal upheaval.

-- •

Enter Cousin Bill, the lawyer. Lillian's husband Luke had trusted Bill so much that Luke had engaged Bill to write his will five years earlier. It was a simple, three-page will. At that time Bill learned how truly rich his Cousin Luke was. Perhaps greed got the better of him, as this was the beginning of Bill's plot to get a piece of that fortune.

Cousin Bill introduced Lillian to David Underhill and Mike Best, two unscrupulous insurance agents who quickly bamboozled the grieving widow into thinking she needed to sell the Berkshire stock. Lillian had met her very own financial serial killers.

No matter the generation, many women live in fear for their financial health. Many depend on their spouse for the larger income. Many have given up their job to raise children, perhaps intending to return to work later. Others are raising children alone—single mothers whose ranks have swollen in recent years. One of the deepest fears held by these vulnerable women is that they may one day wake up destitute, their safety net gone, forced to rely on others for support. They seek out financial guides, preferably in the form of someone they know and can trust.

That is what Lillian thought she had found. When Cousin Bill told Lillian that he could preserve the family wealth, she naturally opened up to him. She had found someone she could trust; who could be more reliable than a family member? And an educated one, with a law degree, at that.

Here we see the natural opening where the con began. This is how their insidious fraud, which netted millions in fees and commissions for the agents and their benefactors at the giant insurance companies, took root and flourished.

Cousin Bill offered his services and those of his law firm after Luke died, when Lillian sought legal advice on administering his estate. He told Lillian to come to the law firm so that they could discuss the couple's Berkshire Hathaway stock, saving accounts, and other assets, which totaled $27 million.

Lillian was still reeling from her husband's death; still in the fog of shock that we all experience when a close family member, particularly a spouse, dies. At their first meeting at Bill's law firm he introduced Lillian to two of his good friends, the insurance agents Best and Underhill. Within minutes the agents recognized their opportunity. This grieving confused widow, with her $24 million in Berkshire Hathaway stock, could land them millions in fees. First they needed to convince Lillian to dump the stock that her husband had held for almost half a century and use the cash proceeds to buy insurance.

• --

When an investor or someone with money like Lillian falls prey to a financial serial killer, the scam usually begins in what appears the most innocent of settings. Perhaps it's over an afternoon cup of coffee at a professional-looking office, or over a steak dinner where the agent or adviser picks up the tab.

-- •

That's how Cousin Bill, along with his buddies Best and Underhill, operated.

The salesmen had a simple but effective and enticing marketing plan. They advertised in local newspapers in Central Texas that they could save families thousands of dollars in estate taxes. DO YOU WANT YOUR ESTATE TO BE PAID OUT IN ESTATE TAXES TO THE GOVERNMENT, OR DO YOU WANT TO PASS YOUR LIFE SAVINGS TO YOUR CHILDREN? read the newspaper ads.

That's a pitch that would catch almost anyone's attention.

There is often a clear and comforting social element to the plan of a financial serial killer. In this case, the ad invited the reader to a free steak dinner at the local Steak & Ale, where Bill, Best, and Underhill would give a complimentary seminar on tax savings. Older Texas residents flocked to the seminars. Who could pass up the opportunity to learn how to save thousands of dollars in estate taxes while enjoying a free steak?

The seminars were mostly attended by seniors, who Underhill later referred to as his "over sixty-five-year-old targets." These "targets" shared a profile. Many were landowners who had held family land for generations but wanted to monetize that asset and pass it on with a minimal tax burden to their children and grandchildren. In Texas, where the individual spirit burns strong, attendees were seeking ways to minimize their tax liabilities and maximize their estates.

Best and Underhill never bought Lillian a steak dinner, but in late 1997, eleven months after her husband's death, they convinced her that it was time to get rid of the Berkshire Hathaway stock.

(Here are a few facts about Berkshire Hathaway. Financial experts regard it as simply the best-run and most diversified mutual fund in the world. It's managed by one of the richest men in the world and the most successful investor ever, Warren Buffett. Buffett, in addition to running his stunningly successful business ventures, also dabbles in advising presidents about the economy in times of crisis.)

"Forget about Buffett, the Oracle of Omaha," Best and Underhill in essence told Lillian. Lillian's estate-planning problems would be solved by purchasing costly doses of life insurance and annuities.

Underhill's version of financial planning shows spectacular disregard for anything other than the products by which he made his career and a handsome living. The man loved—and still loves—life insurance as much as some people in Texas love the Dallas Cowboys.

But Underhill played his game seven days a week, not just on Sundays. He sold insurance with the drive of a quarterback running his offense for a game-winning touchdown.

Underhill's partner, Best, shared much of his zeal, but appeared less fervent. An agent for almost twenty years for a company called Catholic Life Insurance, Best moved to San Antonio in 1990 where he met his new next-door neighbor, Underhill.

After the introduction from Cousin Bill, the two insurance agents set their plot in motion, and landed millions in commissions and fees from Lillian. This is how they did it.

First, Underhill and Best convinced Lillian (who was later deemed senile by one of the same insurance companies who sold her policies) that her heirs would pay a whopping amount of estate taxes on her treasured Berkshire stock unless she sold it.

To avoid the tax, she needed to buy insurance and annuities and put the new investment in something called a family limited partnership.

Underhill and Best had one thing right: family limited partnerships are prudent vehicles for wealthy people to delay paying estate taxes. They work this way: if a family member dies, the other partners—in this case her son Luke Jr.—owes the tax, but can pay it at some later date.

What they did not tell her was that she simply could have paid a law firm about $10,000 to create such a partnership, and then transfer every single share of the Berkshire stock into the new entity. Problem solved, at a reasonable price.

• --

An essential element of the con artist's image is sounding like they have the answer—a true silver bullet—to a person's financial problem. Often the agent will create a sense of urgency to speed the transaction.

-- •

Now the two insurance agents stressed the urgency of the matter, and reassured Lillian they possessed the specialized knowledge necessary to avoid these debilitating estate taxes. Best and Underhill convinced Lillian that without their estate plan, the inheritance taxes due upon her death and her son's death would wipe out the majority of the Wentz family estate.

That, quite simply, was a lie. The scheme was devious: the two agents created a poorly managed family limited partnership and forced Lillian into a completely unnecessary transaction that cost her millions.

To the financial serial killer, each transaction can be justified. The agents never doubted their decision to sell the stock. "We were trying to still pass the complete estate as close as possible intact to the family," Underhill said in a court deposition four years after Lillian's death.

Selling Lillian more than $20 million in insurance and annuities was so important to Best and Underhill that they videotaped a home movie with their biggest and most important client to prove that she was competent and in good health. Some insurance companies require such a video to observe and evaluate a prospective policyholder.

Knowing that Lillian was eighty-nine years old, and possibly in frail health, the insurance companies wanted a videotaped interview of her. They wanted to decide for themselves whether she was in good shape. Best, accompanied by Cousin Bill, visited Lillian to conduct the interview.

That videotape provides a window into the smooth, slick technique of the insurance con man.

Physically, Lillian, wearing pearl earrings and the bright blue dress that she wears to church, looks fine. Her hair is done up. She beams when Best and Bill arrive to see her. Bill holds the camera as Best introduces Lillian in the small breakfast room of her modest country home, which was valued at $55,000, or 0.2 percent of her total assets.

"We have the honor of being in Mrs. Wentz's home," Best tells the camera. "We want to show our underwriters what a lovely lady Mrs. Wentz is."

Lillian tells Best the story about her husband acquiring the Berkshire stock in the 1940s, before Warren Buffett took the helm. She reminds him that the stock is her most important treasure and that she wants to pass it on to her grandchildren. During their discussion, Best nods and chuckles for the camera, feigning interest in her personal mementos and family history. Lillian believes him; she comes from a small town and lacks the guile of the insurance salesman. "Okay, okay," Best keeps repeating, as she hands him papers and newspaper clippings. "Okay, okay. I bet you had the loveliest house in town."

Lillian is so pleased to have visitors. The recorded scene is so warm that you can almost smell the cookies baking in the oven.

One interesting thing about the videotape: it's clearly been edited. It's chopped up. It appears that Best took the liberty of cutting out portions of the tape. Were those the moments where Lillian wandered off in conversation and forgot what she was saying? Where her old age was apparent? Where she couldn't remember simple facts about her life? Where her dementia, from which one doctor said she was suffering, became apparent? We will never know.

The videotaped visit ends with Lillian taking Best into her living room to show him her photo albums. She recounts her happy memories from fifty and sixty years ago. She reminisces about her youth, the Depression, her first job as a schoolteacher, and her early married years. She is so eager to share these memories with her visitor Best.

Best comes across in the videotape as impatient, bored, and obviously ready to leave. He wants to go home. The sale has been made. He's convinced Lillian to sell her stock and buy insurance from him.

Despite the tape, the insurance companies had ample notice of Lillian's poor mental status. Indeed, her "poor memory, poor hearing and problem [with] comprehension" were stated on her application to one giant company and documented on the medical examiner's report.

Best concludes his interview by laying on the charm. "For a lady that's going to be ninety years old in a couple of days, you look about ten or twenty years younger than that," Best tells Lillian. She laughs.

Any investment professional knows that life insurance is essentially worthless to an elderly rich person. Life insurance is meant to provide money to the surviving heirs of the policyholder. Lillian already had over $24 million in Berkshire Hathaway stock to pass on to her heirs; she hardly needed life insurance. In Lillian's case, the premiums on the life insurance policies were so extraordinary, they simply didn't make sense.

The two agents pocketed more than $2 million in fees and commissions.

Best and Underhill did not leave Lillian or her heirs penniless. What they did, however, was to force an unnecessary sale of a shining asset, Berkshire Hathaway stock. Their scheme caused Lillian to make a needless financial transaction that cost her estate, and her heirs, millions of dollars in fees and losses.

The fact that the two agents were so eager to make the $20.5 million sale does not come as a surprise. With firms routinely sponsoring sales contests, big producing agents or stockbrokers are routinely awarded prizes such as plaques, watches, and even vacations. According to Underhill, a top-selling agent, life insurance companies actually have a side business making the awards: "Like most insurance companies, [Standard] owns plaque companies, so we get lots of plaques," he said in his deposition. "I mean, I've got boxes of them."

Life insurance and annuities are one of the highest commission paying financial products. With huge upfront commissions and trailing annual commissions in excess of 6 percent, these products far surpass the commissions paid to brokers who sell stocks or bonds.

The insurance companies should have heard alarm bells and sirens go off in 1997 when Underhill and Best submitted Lillian's policy applications. Most companies prohibit the sale of insurance products to anyone over seventy or eighty, fully recognizing that older people will pay ridiculously high premiums. The sale of such products to the elderly is also prohibited because older people are considered more susceptible to sales frauds. Because of Lillian's age, the insurance companies had to grant special exemptions for the policies, overriding the prohibition of selling insurance to people over eighty years old.

Because Lillian's life insurance policies were so incredibly large, no one underwriter would take on the entire case. Best and Underhill hustled to cobble together a plan to spread the policies among a number of companies since no one firm would underwrite a life insurance policy of more than $20 million. These were not fly-by-night companies, but some of the oldest and most influential financial institutions in the United States. In the case of one firm, Lillian's policy was the largest individual life insurance transaction it had ever made.

In 2001, Lillian's son, Luke Jr., died, and about six months later she passed away. Her three grandsons discovered the family treasure had been lifted, and events had been put into motion where their family wealth was working for insurance agents and companies—not for them. The family sued to recover their lost treasure.

Like many financial frauds, this was a transaction solely for the purpose of a transaction. A transaction took place not to benefit Lillian, but to enrich the agents. The trial, with the Wentz family suing Best, Underhill, and a number of insurance companies, began in January 2006. It was nine years since Lillian's husband Luke died, and almost five years since she had passed when the trial began. So the case was pursued at trial by Lillian's heirs: her daughter-in-law and three adult grandsons.

The Wentz family charged that the insurance agents and carriers gave terrible advice and that the insurance products and annuities were not necessary for the estate plan. The defense argued that the sale of stock was appropriate considering Lillian's age and the fact it made up 85 percent to 90 percent of her wealth. Also, the defense argued that the estate plan did what it was supposed to do, since Lillian and Luke Jr.'s heirs wound up receiving $21 million, and the estate taxes were significantly reduced.

Jury selection began on a Monday morning. The sixty prospective jurors filed into the large ceremonial courtroom and took their seats on the wooden benches. Both sides—the lawyers for Lillian Wentz's family and the insurance company lawyers—surveyed the potential jurors, trying to size them up, before asking them questions to learn which of them could be fair and unbiased.

On the right side of the lawyers' tables at the front of the courtroom sat four Wentz family members, two of their lawyers, and one paralegal. On the left sat more than twenty-five lawyers representing the six insurance companies. This army of lawyers, all dressed in the traditional navy blue or gray legal uniforms, looked overwhelmingly large compared to the tiny legal force assembled by the Wentz family. By all visual measures, this was not going to be a balanced fight.

Questioning of the prospective jurors took place over two days. The Wentz family lawyers were allowed to question the jury panel about their backgrounds, knowledge of insurance, and attitudes toward financial planning. Each group of insurance company lawyers was allowed to do the same. The purpose of this exercise was to try to find twelve jurors who could be fair when hearing the facts of the dispute.

At the end of the questioning by the Wentz family lawyers, one woman seated toward the middle of the assembled group raised her hand. She had a statement she needed to make to the Judge. "Your Honor, I must tell you tell you honestly that I cannot be a fair juror in this case."

"Why?" the judge asked.

"Sir, when I sit here, and I see a mother and her sons sitting on one side of the room and then I look to the other side of the room and I see all those insurance company lawyers, I feel so sorry for her and the fact that she has to try to fight all these big insurance companies."

That woman's sentiments rang loudly in the courtroom. That was the beginning of the end of the fight.

During the next break in the proceedings, the insurance companies began to cave. One insurance company lawyer strode quickly toward the Wentz lawyer, slapped his palms down on the table, and demanded, "We want to settle, and do it now."

Within twenty minutes, a multi-million dollar settlement was negotiated with that company. Once the other companies learned about that settlement, their lawyers began pushing one another aside to try to settle next; no one wanted to be left alone to face the wrath of this jury. Over the next thirty-six hours the Wentz lawyers and the insurance company lawyers held marathon negotiation sessions that resulted in a multi-million dollar payment to the Wentz family.

Postscript

The financial serial killer is never satisfied.

In 2008, a stockbroker from the Midwest called the Wentz family lawyer with questions about Underhill, two years after the lawyer had successfully recovered for the Wentz family its losses. Underhill was making a pitch to the broker's clients—the same pitch that he made to Lillian. He wanted his new targets, a retired couple, to sell $3 million of stock that they had held for years and buy life insurance and annuities. The family's stockbroker thought this was an unnecessary transaction that would benefit the insurance agent more than his clients. After talking to the Wentz family lawyer, the broker persuaded his clients not to follow Underhill's advice.

The Wentz family lawyer was dumbfounded. Hadn't Underhill learned his lesson? Apparently not. Therein lies another insight: the pathological con man can't stop selling. He's an unstoppable bullet train, and he will let no one, and nothing, get in his way.

Lessons & Takeaways

- What is your family treasure? It's probably not a $24 million pot of gold like Lillian's, but it still has great value. Do you understand how to pass your estate, be it a piece of property, a chunk of stock, or your retirement account, to the next generation?
- Money can bring out the worst in people. Be careful. Even family members can turn against family members.
- People are very vulnerable at times of death of close ones, be they spouses, children, parents, lovers, or friends. Be careful of making any immediate decisions, particularly if the professional giving advice is pressuring you to make a decision.
- Con artists can be reputable members or pillars of the community. When it comes to your money, carefully question to whom you give it.
- Cousin Bill was a lawyer. But he betrayed his Aunt Lillian. Credentials and family connections don't always translate to expertise and honesty.

CHAPTER
THREE

The Financial Serial Killer: Charles Ponzi and the Criminal Pathology of White-Collar Thieves

Like Bernie Madoff's crime, many of the frauds that are popping up like financial wildfires across the country are in the form of Ponzi schemes, one of the oldest and most basic rip-offs that endanger investors. Such schemes initially pay unusually high investment returns to investors from the money of new investors—not from any revenue created by a legitimate business.

It's named for Charles Ponzi, an Italian immigrant to the United States, who in 1920 created a massive fraud swapping overseas postal coupons for U.S. stamps. As in many such schemes, the people who invested first made money, luring in later investors who failed to see the fantastic gains.

The Ponzi scheme eventually becomes too big and collapses. Promoters simply cannot raise enough new money to pay investors. Like the thousands of investors recently swindled by Madoff, investors in the original Ponzi scheme mortgaged their homes, put their faith in Ponzi, and then saw their savings completely destroyed. Ponzi was making $250,000 a day—or $2.7 million in today's money—before the scheme collapsed and he went to prison.

After a Ponzi scheme has been discovered and shut down, securities and stock market regulators such as the Securities and Exchange Commission have stated, unsurprisingly, that those running the scheme lavishly spend the stolen money on high-class living. In many ways, these financial serial killers are a predictable group; they rob and then buy fancy cars and homes, charge up tabs in expensive restaurants, and indulge in luxury trips. The Ponzi operator believes that the trappings of the good life are worth the crime.

Ponzi's legacy lives on across the United States today. As stated earlier, the frauds come in a variety of shapes and sizes but all have the same devastating impact.

Financial fraud is so prevalent today, it's talked about at church meetings. Just as Bernie Madoff stole mostly from other Jewish people and a number of Jewish charities and organizations, other religious groups are seeing their members sucked into similar scams. In Utah, a respected Mormon businessman stole $180 million from his fellow members of the Church of Jesus Christ of Latter-Day Saints over the past twenty years, using a Ponzi scheme to commit the largest fraud in the history of the state.

The fraud involving Mormons was so grievous that senior members of the LDS Church in March 2008 warned members to steer clear of financial schemes. In a letter by the church's First Presidency read to its congregations, the church took the extraordinary step to say it was "concerned that there are those who use relationships of trust to promote risky or even fraudulent investment and business schemes."

The church, however, at the time declined to say directly whether the case involving the local businessman, a real estate developer named Val E. Southwick, prompted the warning.

Southwick, sixty-two, reportedly flaunted his Mormon status to help persuade people to invest in phony real estate deals. Southwick was accused of defrauding 800 people from Utah, twenty-nine other states, and three foreign countries of as much as $180 million. Most were members of the LDS church.

The theft eventually caught up with him. He later pleaded guilty to nine felony counts. In June 2008, he received back-to-back prison terms of one to fifteen years for each of the nine charges.

A common theme with these scams is the psychological bond that exists between financial serial killers like Southwick and his victims. Investors often fail to believe that their investment wizard or guru could have any role in hurting them. When investigators in 2006 asked for their help, many of Southwick's victims simply did not cooperate.

Investors often are blind and can't believe—at first, at least—that the financial serial killer stole their money. "This man came to my husband's funeral," a victim might think. "It would be impossible for him to rip me off." Another victim might say to himself, "But this person came to my house and sat down for dinner with me and my wife. There's no way he could want to hurt me."

Too often, such thinking is proven wrong. Instead, the financial serial killer was, in subtle and not so subtle ways, blinding his victims and casting a spell over their common sense. It happens time and time again. Financial serial killers use repetitive techniques, which this book brings to light.

Despite the damage, no one will ever know for certain how much money such Ponzi schemes run by financial serial killers have recently cost the American public. The losses to investors of the Southwick scams listed above totaled $180 million dollars, a staggering amount, but still a drop in the bucket compared to Bernie's $50 billion scam. (That's the figure believed to be missing from client accounts, including the phony, fabricated gains Madoff said he was delivering.)

• --

Investors must be on the look out for an adviser or financial whiz who "promises" or "guarantees" a return in the double digits, especially when the market is spinning downward.

-- •

Many Ponzi scheme artists and financial serial killers promise returns of 15 percent to 20 percent per year, and the plans collapse after two to three years because there are not enough new investors to pay off the old. Madoff, however, said he was generating a 10.5 percent return each year, and managed his fraud for twenty years.

Since the Madoff fraud was revealed in December 2008, a number of other significant frauds have come to light, and public attention has never been more focused on such stories.

In January 2009, the front pages of both the *New York Times* and the *Wall Street Journal* reported on the proliferation of such schemes. Both papers highlighted the exploits of crooked financial adviser Marcus Schrenker, who was on the lam and faked his death by crashing an airplane—only after leaping from it first.

On New Year's Eve 2008, weeks after Madoff admitted to his ruthless scam, officials with the Indiana Secretary of State's office raided Schrenker's home in Fishers, Indiana, seizing computers, cash, files from his money management business, the title to his Lexus, and his passport. Schrenker's personal assets included a $1.7 million home and two private planes. He faced allegations from insurance regulators that he had bilked investors of $250,000 in fees for unnecessarily switching annuities, and was also charged with unlawful acts and unlawful transactions as an adviser. After the raid, Schrenker fled.

The *New York Post*, which regularly features celebrities, sports, and assorted titillations on its front page, found the story so riveting that it pasted the financial adviser on its cover. It's not often that a stockbroker from the Midwest is chosen as the most sensational story of the day, but Schrenker certainly fit the billing. Schrenker and his thin, blonde wife were on the cover of the *Post*'s January 14, 2009, edition. Under the headline CAUGHT!, the couple was pictured in happier, more prosperous times; Schrenker wearing a black suit and gold necktie, and his wife sporting heels and a black cocktail dress that showed off her toned legs, arms, and shoulders. Behind them were the fruits of Schrenker's scheme: a twin-engine airplane and a silver Lexus.

As the *Post* and other national newspapers reported, Schrenker's arrest ended an odyssey that began eleven days after the authorities raided his home. That's when Schrenker, thirty-nine, took off in his private plane from Indianapolis, claiming he was bound for Florida. He radioed a phony distress call over Birmingham,

Alabama, saying his windshield had shattered and he was bleeding profusely.

He then stopped responding to air-traffic controllers, and approaching military jet pilots saw the plane flying with its door open. They didn't realize it at the time, but Schrenker had already jumped from the Piper Malibu, and the aircraft was on autopilot.

After it crashed in a Florida swamp two hours later, rescuers found the windshield undamaged. There was no sign of blood— or Schrenker.

The story then took a turn straight out of a screenwriter's handbook, the *Post* said.

Schrenker emerged from the woods 200 miles away near Childersburg, Alabama, wet from the knees down and wearing aviation goggles, and told authorities he had been in a canoe accident.

Not seeing anything suspicious, police drove him to a nearby motel, where he checked in and soon disappeared. He was last seen running into the woods wearing a black hat. "He didn't leave a mess. He didn't leave anything. He didn't even take a shower," said Yogi Patel, owner of the Harpersville Motel, the *Post* reported.

Later, he appeared at a storage facility seven miles away, where he had stashed a red 2008 Yamaha motorcycle with fully loaded saddlebags. Schrenker ditched his wet clothes in a trash bin and was off.

Hours later, a friend received an e-mail purportedly from Schrenker in which he wrote, "By the time you get this, I'll be gone. I embarrassed my family for the last time."

On August 19, 2009, about eight months after his arrest and subsequent appearance on the front page of a variety of newspapers, Marcus Schrenker was sentenced to four years in prison for charges related to the airplane crash. He faces a variety of other charges that could lead to more time in prison.

The roots of fraud go back centuries. Fraudulent financial transactions that seem almost mystical in their composition and ability to grow but in the end wipe out investors is part of our financial culture, says Professor Larry E. Sullivan, chief librarian for the Lloyd George Sealy Library, which is part of the John Jay College of Criminal Justice in New York. He's an associate dean, too.

Sullivan, sixty-five, has taught courses with titles such as the "Philosophy of Punishment" and "Elite Deviance," and he becomes animated as he discusses the techniques of the financial serial killer. Originally a medieval scholar, he has written or edited nine books on crime and fraud.

There is no esoteric reasoning or understanding the motivation of the financial serial killer, Sullivan says. It comes down to his own greed, and then spotting that greed in others. "I would think that it's because people want to make money. And that's what these types of con men and fraudsters are," people who prey on others' desire and need to make money.

You never know when fraud is going to happen, except that history shows it's going to keep happening, Sullivan says. We can't escape it. Frauds and scams are part of our culture of business. "People want to make money, and they want to do it the easiest way possible." Some of these investors want to make money without working for a living, or, when it comes to some financial professionals, they want to make money from sophisticated financial instruments, like those at the root of the current global economic credit crisis. "When you have speculation you can make a quick buck," he says. Elaborate investment programs that blow up in the end can be a fundamental part of harming investors and destroying their savings.

When it comes to financial serial killers, there's not much new, Sullivan says. What's current is simply variations on timeworn cons or scams. An unusual glimpse of Charles Ponzi can be gained with the recent discovery of an unpublished manuscript by his publicity agent, William McMasters.

McMasters was a preeminent public relations man when he took on Ponzi as a client in July 1920. Ponzi wanted to work with the best. McMasters was a lawyer who had served in the Spanish-American War, and he had handled publicity for the campaigns of several Massachusetts political figures, including Calvin Coolidge and John F. Fitzgerald (President John F. Kennedy's grandfather), the *New York Times* reported in May 2009.

Ponzi was already a convicted felon, though McMasters and the world did not find that out until later. Born in Italy in 1882, he arrived in North America in 1903 and made his way to Montreal, where he served three years for check forgery.

New York Times reporter Ralph Blumenthal gives a full account of the relationship between Ponzi and McMasters:

> Ponzi eventually returned to Boston and devised a novel scheme to build a financial empire based on prepaid coupons that nations issued for postal replies. By buying the coupons at a fixed rate, he could exploit

international currency fluctuations by redeeming them at a higher price.

After offering depositors high interest rates, Ponzi never really dealt in postal coupons, which turned out to be too unwieldy for large-scale speculation. Instead, he just paid off his first depositors with money from later investors who would also have to be repaid. In the end, he was short as much as $10 million—the equivalent of more than $100 million today. He pleaded guilty, was sent to prison, then was deported to Italy and died in Brazil in 1949.

Now, while Ponzi, in his autobiography, barely mentioned McMasters, the publicist undeniably played a role in his unraveling—a greater role, according to McMasters, than previously acknowledged.

After being hired by Ponzi, McMasters said he arranged an exclusive interview with the striving financier in *The Boston Post,* since defunct but then one of the largest-selling morning newspapers in the country. Ponzi's promised high rates were already drawing eager investors, but a front-page splash on July 24, 1920, under the headline DOUBLES THE MONEY WITHIN THREE MONTHS, aroused a frenzy. Privately, though, McMasters was beginning to have his doubts. "I have never heard of such steady returns on any investment," he wrote.

Later, poring over records, McMasters said he realized that "the only money [Ponzi] had in his hands as of right now was money taken from investors," adding, "The huge profits that he discussed so glibly were mythical and nonexistent."

"Once I had reached that conclusion," he continued, "I knew that I was faced with a duty that I owed to the public if I expected to stay in business for the rest of my life." That night, he said, "I decided to write the exposé of his fantastic story."

He offered the story to Richard Grozier, the *Post*'s general manager and assistant publisher, asking him, "How would you like to have a story blowing [Ponzi] up sky high?" The newspaper wavered. In an unusual move, McMasters said, he secretly secured a promise from Nathan Tufts, the district attorney where Grozier lived, to provide the publisher immunity from prosecution "in case the story turned out to be untrue and libelous."

Over the objections of the city editor, Grozier gave Mr. McMasters the go-ahead, arranging to pay him $5,000 for the article plus a $1,000 bonus if all turned out well—the huge sum (the equivalent of $64,000 today), according to the publicist, payable in cash so as to be untraceable if the story backfired.

With the blaring headline, DECLARES PONZI IS NOW HOPELESSLY INSOLVENT, Mr. McMasters's article dominated the front page on August 2, 1920, sealing Ponzi's fate, especially after the *Post* unearthed Ponzi's criminal record in Montreal a week later.

"It was a nail in the coffin," said Ponzi biographer Mitchell Zuckoff, noting that other reporters had also begun chipping away at Ponzi's scheme.

Ponzi's fantastic returns kindled suspicions in McMasters, and claims of such fantastic returns should arouse the suspicions of the average investor, Professor Sullivan and many others warn.

If someone claims he is investing your money and getting a return of 20 percent a year, you should know that's impossible, Sullivan says. "Something's got to be wrong." Investors hate to face up to reality, he says. "But you don't want to believe that, do you, because you are making the 20 percent a year."

Ponzi schemes are simple, and therefore alluring to both the financial serial killer and the investor. The scheme depends on more money coming in all the time. Greed motivates the Ponzi operator, and fabulous returns certainly can blind and seduce the investor.

Ponzi created the blueprint for this type of scam, and con men like Madoff have followed it ever since.

"Like many confidence men, Ponzi preyed on his own kind, and the Boston Italian community embraced him with delirious joy," wrote Ron Chernow, the noted biographer of Alexander Hamilton and John D. Rockefeller in the *New Yorker* a few months after Madoff told the world he was a fraud. "Ponzi was convinced that he was a wizard who had stumbled upon a form of financial alchemy that had eluded answers. Incapable of moral clarity, he could never quite admit to himself that he was a charlatan and that his scheme was an impossible fiasco. He fooled others because he fooled himself. Right up until the end, he found refuge in fantasies that he might take over a chain of banks or shipping lines that would enable him to pay off his legions of worshipful investors. He never suffered serious remorse or second thoughts."

Chernow notes Madoff and others since 1920 have taken elements of Ponzi's scam and enhanced them. "Madoff imitated

Ponzi in a few particulars, such as victimizing his own community (in his case, Jewish), and inventing fictitious returns, but his improvements on the traditional Ponzi scheme are breathtaking.

"Where Ponzi pandered to uneducated investors and promised gargantuan returns, Madoff trimmed annual returns to a modest but wondrously reliable eight to twelve percent," Chernow wrote. "Madoff's seductive appeal lay not so much in his purported profits as in his consistency. Wealthy investors could flatter themselves that, far from being greedy, they were sacrificing yield for security. Madoff's method enabled him to swindle rich people who prided themselves on their financial conservatism and sophistication, enabling him to appeal to an avarice of a quiet, upper-crust sort."

Chernow asks if Madoff intended from the outset to create such a fraud. To answer the question, he compares Madoff with another swindler, Ivan Kreuger, "a Swedish financier of the 1920s and the operator of a global safety match business so enormous that he was dubbed the Match King."

The two had some remarkable similarities, Chernow concludes. Madoff and Kreuger were both "colorless and unassuming." Both created a "mystique by playing hard to get and retreating into a tight little zone of secrecy."

Kreuger "aroused exaggerated expectations of [profits] he couldn't live up to," Chernow wrote. In 1932, his company was desperate for credit and more funds from investors, but, in the middle of the Great Depression, his backers on Wall Street had shut him off. That March, Kreuger shot himself in Paris.

Kreuger's tale, Chernow concludes, "presents a credible explanation of how giant Ponzi enterprises come about: not as sudden inspirations of criminal masterminds but as the gradual culmination of small moral compromises made by financiers who aren't quite as ingenious as they think."

When Madoff pleaded guilty in March 2009, he explained that at first he believed his fraud was going to be short-lived, Chernow notes.

Professor Sullivan distinguishes between the two types of financial serial killers the public must watch out for. As noted, there are the Madoffs and the Schrenkers, who are thieves and sociopaths.

Another potentially more dangerous type is the genius who believes in his mathematical models for investing more than practical reality warrants. Maybe he's not a financial serial killer in the sense that he will knowingly and consciously prey on a victim, but his belief in his system and the hubris attached to it in the face of reality can do great harm to investors.

The recent global banking and credit crisis, which was tied to the real estate bubble, shows that investors can also be harmed by professional investors who believe they have cracked the code to investing and act with the utmost hubris.

In 2007, the real estate "bubble had begun to deflate," noted James Stewart of the *New Yorker* in an analysis of the collapse, the leading players, and how it changed Wall Street. "Defaults among subprime-mortgage borrowers rose, and then the elaborate infrastructure of mortgage-backed securities started to erode."

In a credit crisis, there is a sudden and swift reduction in the availability of loans or credit. It also occurs when banks suddenly tighten restrictions on businesses, institutions, and individuals. The result is disastrous. For example, if a company can't borrow cash for short periods of time, it could mean they fail to have the money in hand to pay their workers while the company itself waits to get paid for delivering merchandise.

Professor Sullivan stresses that our recent crisis has been played out before. "Look at the early eighteenth century. In 1719 and 1720 it was John Law and the Mississippi bubble." That's when Law, a Scottish economist who wound up testing his economic theories as controller general of France, created an asset bubble in which shares of a private company were traded for government debt. The shares in the company were used like a paper currency. Like the securities and derivatives tied to the housing market, the John Law investments inflated fantastically in a very short period of time. In that scheme, it all crashed when large groups of investors tried to cash in their shares.

"Throughout history, you have these cycles," Sullivan says. "I'm a cynic who believes there always is a greed involved. People don't want to face reality. If it's too good to be true, it isn't true. That's the point. But people don't quite want to believe that."

Financial disasters have occurred for centuries, but they take different forms and show variations, he says. Investors need to be on their guard more than ever before. "It's a little more sophisticated now."

Today, investment firms, banks, and hedge funds use mathematical models to determine how to invest. "We're supposed to think that it's the gospel truth. But you still have people involved, that's why I think behavioral economics should be considered when investing."

Behavioral economics and finance uses scientific research on human social, cognitive, and emotional factors to understand how people make economic decisions and use money. It also examines the impact those decisions have on markets and the returns on investments. Simply put, "that's human psychology," Sullivan says.

The mania around making money has been studied for centuries, yet investors still fall prey to schemes. Sullivan points to the nineteenth-century critique, *Extraordinary Popular Delusions and the Madness of Crowds*, as one such analysis. The book examines how and why groups of people commit massive acts of collective idiocy, particularly around investment manias.

The investors' coercion begins with simply the lure of making money, Sullivan says. The pitch is simple. "I'm going to let you in on a deal—because I made money. Like with Madoff. So you beg to get in—and you have this type of hysteria. You get in and make some money." The desire to be part of the experience can be overwhelming, he says. "You simply don't want to lose out."

The Internet stock bubble of 1998–2000, in which technology companies' stock market value was based on growth instead of real profits, also had a devastating effect on investors.

The dot-com crash wiped out $5 trillion in market value of technology companies between March 2000 and October 2002. For example, the share price of eToys went from the $80 reached during its IPO in May 1999 to less than $1 when it declared bankruptcy in February 2001. Boo.com was a typically spectacular failure. It spent $188 million in just six months in an attempt to create a global online fashion store and went bankrupt in May 2000.

"None of these companies were making any money," Sullivan says. "In fact they were in debt, but their stock prices were going sky-high." A few notables have survived and become part of our everyday culture, such as Google and Amazon, but those companies are the real exceptions to the Internet bubble, he notes.

Before they put their savings at risk or invest money set aside for their children's college education, investors should simply slow down, take stock, and get answers to simple questions. "A warning sign [of a bubble] is whether the company is making any money at all. Does the company have any real earnings? Investors must ask and try to figure out, 'Why is your stock so damn high?'"

"Then of course, there are the mathematical geniuses with the hedge funds—like Long Term Capital Management—saying you can't fail," Sullivan says.

Long Term Capital Management was a hedge fund founded in 1994 by the former vice chairman and head of bond trading at Salomon Brothers. On its board sat two scholars who share the 1997 Nobel Memorial Prize in Economic Sciences. During its first five years, the fund was enormously successful, and had annualized returns of over 40 percent, after fees. The fund exploded in 1998 when its managers made a bet on the direction of a foreign currency. The fund lost $4.6 billion, was bailed out by Wall Street banks, and folded in early 2000.

Beware of the investment professional who promises a new paradigm or new model.

Watch out for those investment professionals who believe that "there's always a new paradigm," Sullivan says. "Always be cautious of guys who pitch a foolproof, can't fail, mathematical model. But those guys at Long Term Capital Management really believed in it. They kind of thought that they couldn't fail. On the other hand, you've got the Madoffs, who know they're frauds."

The failure of Long Term Capital Management did not deter its principals. Many joined together and began another hedge fund operation. That second fund lost 44 percent from September 2007 to February 2009. It was shut down in the summer of 2009.

Sullivan points to Warren Buffett, the famous investor who created Lillian Wentz's fortune, who has preached he would never invest in a business he didn't understand. "I agree with Buffett—if you can't understand what the hell they're doing don't invest with them," Sullivan says.

Most investors don't want to take history into account when thinking about their savings: "People don't really want to look at the reality of or the history of these financial markets, nor even think about the bubbles throughout history," Sullivan says.

Instead, Americans continue to live in a culture in which hype is confused with solid information and the wild belief that striking it rich is just an investment or two away, Sullivan says. Cable news shows and the Internet can contribute to such blindness.

Commentators who tout stocks are part of that cultural problem, Sullivan says.

For example, Jim Cramer, a former hedge fund manager and current CNBC commentator, has a varied record in the investment business. As a hedge fund manager, he had a wildly successful career. Cramer's fund had one down year from 1988-2000. In 1999 the fund returned 47 percent; in 2000 28 percent, beating the Standard & Poor's 500 stock index by 38 percentage points.

He's also made some oddball calls and some outright doozies. He touted former Major League Baseball All-Star Lenny Dykstra as a "legend" of investing. In July 2009, Dykstra filed for bankruptcy.

As the credit crisis threatened to bring the entire economy to a halt in September 2008, Cramer stepped in it.

He recommended to his audience that they should buy Wachovia stock days before it collapsed in September 2008 and was scooped up by Wells Fargo at a bargain price, leaving Wachovia shareholders pennies per share.

On September 15, 2008, Cramer invited the CEO of Wachovia, Robert Steele, on his show, *Mad Money*, in order to recommend the stock to potential investors. Cramer agreed with Steele that the company was fundamentally sound and that the ratio of good loans to bad loans was low. "Thanks to the leadership of Bob Steele, who I believe will be able to split [Wachovia] into a good bank and a bad bank, and lead it much higher."

A few months later, Wachovia no longer existed. By the end of the year, Wachovia was forced into a merger with rival Wells Fargo.

The appetite for such hype leaves Sullivan in disbelief. "And people are still watching Cramer," Sullivan says. "I think that with cable news too—you've got too many people like that telling you what to do."

How and why you believe, particularly when it comes to money, is just as important as what you believe in, Sullivan says. "When it comes to money and investing, you need to be very conscious of what you are investing your faith into, as well."

People can be dangerously naive when dealing with con men, Sullivan says. Such fraudsters have a personality that will entice you to give them money. Urgency is often a signal of a con artist at work, he says. The transaction must be completed immediately, like someone who's trying to sell you a used car.

"They've got to close the deal right away and I never do that. I never give money over the phone. It's impulsive. The pitch is, 'This is the deal I'm going to give you right now. If you walk you're not going to get it.'" That strikes an investor's impulse. "This happens all the time," Sullivan notes.

Investors must ask questions if they want to avoid the scam, Sullivan says. "I can understand people investing with [Madoff] because they're making big returns and they just don't want to look at reality, they don't want to ask, 'What is he doing with the money? How is he getting the 10.5 percent return when the stock market had a big dip recently?'"

Lessons & Takeaways

- The history of investing is filled with bubbles, hype, and outrageous promises. In investing, don't get caught up in hype and hysteria.
- There is no new paradigm or new economy. Those are just buzzwords used to entice you into an investment that is new and has no history of success.
- No market trend, up or down, lasts forever.
- The investment guru who has a secret method of making riches could well be a flimflam man.
- Is your investment adviser too perfect? Like Madoff, is he or she generating returns that, year in, year out, closely resemble each other? Be especially suspicious if these returns are being achieved when the overall market is going down and other professional investors are losing money.
- If an investment looks too good to be true, it probably is.

CHAPTER
FOUR

Bre-X Minerals: How to Make, and Detect, Fool's Gold

When the economy faces huge questions and uncertainty, the prices for precious metals can take off because investors want what's perceived as a safe haven, something tangible and real they can hold on to. With recent global economic instability and the weakening of the U.S. dollar, gold has reached record prices of well over $1,000 an ounce. As gold prices spike to record highs, it's time to revisit one of the greatest gold scams ever, so that we can learn from it and see if investors are vulnerable to such frauds right now.

Gold is unique because it glitters, it captures the imagination, and it kindles greed like nothing else, even more than a roaring stock. At this precarious moment in the U.S. and global economy, gold scamsters will be coming for you. All you have to do is listen to AM radio or watch late-night cable television to hear the latest gold offerings.

The *appearance* of legitimacy is a key part to any scam, and is essential to a gold or mining scam. In a fraud, the smoke screen of legitimacy is sometimes so dense and dark that investors, along with professionals such as bankers and journalists, simply fail to see through the fog.

One of the biggest gold scams of all time had such layers of bogus legitimacy. In 1995 Bre-X Minerals Ltd., a Canadian mining company, declared it had discovered the biggest deposit of gold ore in history in Busang, Indonesia, on the island of Borneo.

• --

Watch out for the hyperbole of the con man or group con—hype and fizzy talk of riches can be enticing, but be on full alert if something is pitched to you as being the *biggest* and *best* deal ever.

-- •

Bre-X appeared to have an outstanding pedigree. It had been endorsed by analysts at the largest and best-known Wall Street investment banks and journalists from respected news organizations. The mine drew the intense interest of the Indonesian government and the adult children of the country's dictator, Suharto, as well as from legitimate mining companies in Canada and the United States—all vying to control Bre-X because of its supposed gold discovery.

Intense greed surrounded the gold mine, which only appeared to grow larger over time. After the site was first explored in 1995 the company said it discovered at least 2.3 million ounces of gold. The next year, that number shot up to 30 million ounces, and then shortly thereafter that doubled to 60 million ounces. Finally, in 1997, the company announced the discovery had grown to 70 million ounces. The shareholders saw the company's stock value top $4 billion in September 1996, for a growth rate of 100,000 percent in three years.

It all came tumbling down just a few months later when the stock price evaporated in March 1997. The Indonesian government had dispatched an independent mining company to verify the enormous find, but their tests showed that there was no gold in the ground. The claim of a vast discovery underground had been one gigantic hoax.

Four specific contributors buttressed the con: Bre-X's large and impressive mining operations, the news media, investment banks, and the mining industry. Each played a significant role in convincing investors the wonderland of Bre-X was real.

The Bre-X exploration camp on the Indonesian island of Borneo was a bustling enterprise with an army of workers. The site had been cleared deep in the jungle and buildings erected where the forest once stood. There were barracks that served as home to hundreds of workers, from miners to geologists. Alongside them was a commissary, a testing laboratory, and a geology room housing the maps that marked the locations of the hidden treasure below the ground. In addition to this setup were the trucks, drilling rigs, and tools of the mining trade. The company had even carved "Bre-X" into a huge swath of grass to mark the operation site. The size and the physicality of the place were extremely convincing parts of the fraud.

Bre-X received a tremendous boost from the press, and this proved to be vital to the success of the fraud.

The media were enchanted with the story of the upstart mining company that stumbled upon one of the largest gold finds in history. The story had all the rags-to-riches elements that journalists look for. The founder and president of Bre-X, David

Walsh, personified the Horatio Alger qualities of a man who began working in his basement, then through hard work and a little luck made the record-setting discovery.

Walsh himself was the consummate promoter. He fiercely defended his company against anyone who doubted its discovery. He wrote up the early press releases for the company. He knew how to work the hype. At his core he was a promoter, a gambler, and a hustler.

On reflection, the involvement of Walsh alone should have raised red flags. He was a former stockbroker who started Bre-X in 1989. He searched for both gold and diamonds in the Northwest Territories of Canada, but had no luck. He filed for personal bankruptcy, took the last of his money and flew to Indonesia. There he met up with an old friend, John Felderhof, who seemed to have the knack for finding minerals deep under the ground, and the two of them raised some money to buy a plot of land on the island of Borneo in 1993. Walsh and Felderhof invited Michael de Guzman, a Filipino geologist, to join their team. After some exploring on Borneo, they discovered the Busang gold site.

Walsh ensured positive press for the company by targeting young reporters and sending them his press releases. The journalists who took the bait were generally inexperienced and hungry for a good story that could make their name. One young reporter later expressed regret for his role in promoting the scam.

He had not been skeptical of the Bre-X story at all; he felt that he was getting a break because this company called *him* and said that they had found a huge gold discovery. He had done no independent investigation to determine whether the story was true, yet wrote the story and sent it out to the news wires. In retrospect, he realized that he was a pawn in the Bre-X plan, and that he helped fuel the manic pumping up of the stock.

Other sources of information reinforced the Bre-X claims of its Indonesian El Dorado. Investors often rely on newsletters to learn more information about a company. There are thousands of newsletters that cover certain stocks—and there are newsletters that cover the mining industry. Walsh and his team cozied up with the people who publish these supposedly independent newsletters.

Many of these industry newsletters hyped the Bre-X story. In 1993, one of these newsletters, *Carter's Choice*, wrote about a little company that had made some "very promising" gold discoveries. The author of *Carter's Choice* told his readers that he himself had bought some stock in the company.

What the author of the newsletter failed to divulge was that he had known David Walsh for many years; that Walsh was his old drinking buddy, and that Walsh had a terrible track record in the mining industry. After the collapse, the *Carter's Choice* editor told one writer that he considered Walsh to be a "heavy drinker" who "never appeared destined for great success." Unfortunately for Bre-X investors, this side of Walsh was never revealed while the stock was being hyped.

The mining and metals industry helped boost Bre-X's tremendous credibility. In 1996, gold fever surrounding Bre-X was intensifying, and large multinational companies started to show interest in buying out the company because of the massive gold deposits. Executives from companies such as Barrick Gold, the world's second largest gold producer, and Placer Dome flew to Indonesia to find a way to buy Bre-X and gain control of the biggest gold discovery in the history of the world. Barrick hired private detectives to dig up dirt on Bre-X in order to launch a hostile takeover of the company. Barrick even enlisted former President George H.W. Bush to lobby Indonesian dictator Suharto, and retained Suharto's daughter as a consultant to get an edge in the Bre-X takeover attempt.

The crowd on Wall Street cheered Bre-X on.

The big Wall Street investment banks analyzed the stock and issued written recommendations to buy Bre-X shares. Lehman Brothers analysts claimed to have visited the Bre-X gold mining site on Borneo. They reported that they had personally observed the gold operations, and wrote a series of highly detailed analyses, including descriptions of independent testing that had been performed on core samples taken from the mines. The analysts highly recommended the shares, right up to a few months before the company collapsed.

The Busang gold discovery "is enormous," Lehman wrote in a report to investors in December 1996. Lehman expected this "growth story to continue in a major way for the rest of this decade." The Lehman analyst, Daniel McConvey, was well-regarded in the industry. A former employee of Barrick Gold, McConvey traveled to the Busang gold site to make an on-the-scene inspection. He called it "the find of the century."

Another analyst, Bob Sibthorpe of Yorkton Securities, wrote: "Arriving at a final gold resource number for Busang is difficult since the deposit is beyond the scope of anything seen to date. . . . A visit to the property is necessary to grasp the magnitude of what is going on and to justify throwing out the rule book." Yet another claimed that "the Busang deposit will continue to grow," although he gave no basis for this grandiose prediction. An analyst at J.P. Morgan & Co., David Neuhaus, made the most outlandish prediction when he proclaimed, "I'd say 150 million ounces is a conservative guess as to what Bre-X will ultimately come up with" at the Busang mine. It comes as no surprise that two months later, J.P. Morgan was anointed as one of Bre-X's new financial advisers.

Among all these glowing reports that exhorted investors to load up on the stock, not a single analyst reported that he had ever independently tested the soil for gold. Each analyst had taken Walsh and Felderhof at their word verifying their claims.

At the Busang site, analysts had gathered in a small map room where Felderhof reviewed the drilling results. He pointed out the drill holes and described how they were turning up incredible grades of gold. After gold samples were pulled from the ground they were sent to a gold testing lab about an hour from the site.

None of the major Wall Street houses were willing to ruin this party. Bre-X was growing, the stock was soaring, and there was money to be made from several angles. Bre-X needed the investment banks to help it raise money, and large fees would follow. Clients were getting richer by the day as the stock continued to climb. The last thing any analyst wanted to do was question these claims of expanding gold finds. That could lead to investors dumping the stock, which in turn would trigger declining stock prices, lost fortunes, and ultimately a company that could no longer afford to pay its bankers. A negative report, or one that questioned the company's claims, could potentially cause Bre-X to deny banking business to the violator.

Lehman, J.P. Morgan, and the other Wall Street titans were motivated by the fees that they earned, or hoped to earn, from underwriting and trading Bre-X stock. The analysts who work for these firms are paid from the profits generated from all this banking activity, providing them with an incentive to be optimistic about a company that is paying them fees.

J.P. Morgan was Bre-X's key financial adviser at the time of the collapse. In February 1997, weeks before the collapse, J.P. Morgan bankers talked up the Busang mine in a conference call during which Bre-X's top geologist predicted the deposit could contain a staggering 150 million ounces of gold, worth $70 billion at the time. Despite these astonishing forecasts, industry watchers continued to buy in to the story.

Indirectly, and likely without knowing it, many Main Street investors owned a piece of Bre-X. The company's shares were bought by top mutual funds, the most common and popular way for people to invest in the stock market. Fidelity Investments, at the time the world's biggest mutual fund company, owned 7.3 percent of Bre-X at the end of 1996.

> The media, brokerage firms and investment newsletters play a large role in the hype of a stock.

As gold fever emanating from Busang mounted, some investors in Bre-X were growing apprehensive. A group of investors hired me, coauthor Tom Ajamie, to act as its watchdog. The group wanted me to make sure Bre-X was serving the interest of its longtime shareholders, many of whom had bought the stock for pennies.

I made several trips to Indonesia, at the stockholders' request, to try to speak to Bre-X management and government officials who had authority over the company. For years, the top executives at Bre-X had been extremely accessible to these investors, fielding their phone calls, meeting with them regularly, and giving updates about the company's progress. At the time I was hired, this shareholder group had begun having difficulty getting the Bre-X management to return their phone calls. After having been so open for years, management was clamming up—sending a red flag to the investors.

Rumors were spreading that Indonesian dictator Suharto and two of his children wanted a piece of the action. The investors wanted to make sure that Bre-X remained independent and was not taken over by the Indonesian government, or sold for a pittance to a rival mining company. They wanted to protect their investment in the stock, which was worth millions.

These investors were paying attention to their investment, keeping an eye on the activities of the company, and taking proactive measures to protect their investment. One would say that they were really doing everything right. They never imagined that they were about to lose everything and fall victim to a huge con.

The Bre-X scam began to fall apart in early 1997. In late January, as one mining company was about to seize control of the project, a fire destroyed a map room at Busang containing all the geologists' records.

My first trip to Indonesia was over the Christmas and New Year's holiday in 1996. I went a second time a few weeks later in January 1997. Over a period of several weeks I interviewed government mining officials, mining industry executives, journalists, and others who could shed some light on the Bre-X phenomenon and reveal information about this historic discovery. I was trying to determine, for my clients, whether the Bre-X mine would be acquired by a major mining company or be taken over by the Indonesian government. The Indonesian government had delayed giving Bre-X complete control over the site. The major mining companies were jockeying to be selected as the operator— or owner—of the operation.

Senior government mining officials agreed to meet with me. Those meetings took place in the lobby bars of five-star hotels in the capital city of Jakarta. These glittering hotels are the cleanest and most exclusive meeting places in Jakarta, a city of almost 10 million people that is plagued by pollution and squalor. Stray cats and dogs run alongside bumper-to-bumper cars and motorized *tuk-tuks* that creep along the narrow, jammed roadways. The smell of exhaust is overwhelming. The scene in Jakarta is one of constant chaos, desperation, and danger.

Nothing is what is seems. Two government officials agreed to meet with me to discuss Bre-X. The men arrived at my hotel wearing traditional *batik* shirts of muted brown. They reeked of the omnipresent clove cigarettes. They spoke in riddles, saying Bre-X might remain independent but then it might not. They wanted to know what I knew about the discovery and pumped me for information. Did I know what the major mining companies were planning? Could I verify the amount of gold in the ground at the mine? What was the value of the mine? After a little while I realized that these government representatives— who were deans of the Indonesian mining department—either knew very little about the Bre-X discovery or knew a lot but would never reveal it.

The government angle took another odd turn when I was visited at my hotel room by someone who claimed to be its representative. The insider looked me straight in the eye and told me to leave the country now or risk being killed. This made no sense. It seemed odd that asking questions about a gold mine would engender this type of threat. When a second messenger arrived the next day to deliver the same warning, I decided it was time to change hotels and use a different name.

I also realized that I needed to be more cautious in my investigative activities. The bearers of this threatening news had somehow learned my hotel and room number. I recounted the threats to some American friends in the local press corps. They told me that the Indonesian government had eyes and spies everywhere, and that it cost only a few thousand rupiah (the equivalent of one dollar) to pay off someone working at the front desk of a hotel. Such a small "tip" would yield a fully printed copy of my hotel charges and a duplicate key to my room.

The information that couldn't be bought from the hotel clerks could be purchased from any cabdriver who had taken me from here to there. My skin color and dress tagged me immediately as a foreigner. I was someone who should be watched carefully, and whose monitored activities could command a price. Indonesia is a country of over 240 million people, where nearly half of the population lives on less than $2 per day. Hiring a network of spies might cost $40 per week. It was likely that my movements were being watched and reported.

To keep up my investigation while trying not to anger the wrong people I decided to shift into counterespionage mode. I would take a cab halfway to my destination and then pay the driver to drop me off. I would hail a second cab to shuttle me to my destination. That way no single cab driver would know where I started and ended.

Most documents that I received would eventually need to be shredded. I had no shredder in my hotel room. Even if I could have acquired one, it would really be of no effective use. I recalled vividly the stories of the insurgent students who during the Iranian Revolution in 1979 had stormed the U.S. embassy in Iran and took Americans hostage. The occupying Iranians had gathered up all the scraps of shredded classified documents that U.S. embassy personnel had left behind. The Iranians enlisted local carpet weavers who then painstakingly pieced the documents back together by hand over a number of years. The Iranians were then able to read the reams of classified documents that our embassy had seemingly stored and destroyed in confidence.

Every hotel room has a device that is much more effective than a shredder. It's what we commonly refer to as a toilet. I ripped up all the most sensitive papers daily, and flushed them. They commingled with the contents of the hundreds of other flushing commodes in the hotel and were swept away to a sewage depot somewhere far afield.

The government angle was proving to be unfruitful, and a little dangerous. So I set my sights on trying to talk to some of the Bre-X management that was ensconced at the ritzy Shangri-La hotel. They were holed up there to discuss a possible sale of the company to one of the major mining companies. Despite repeated visits to the hotel and numerous phone calls, Bre-X management refused to speak to me. Again, this was somewhat strange considering that I was representing major shareholders who, until just a few months ago, had been able to call management and speak to them directly.

Next in line for interviews were some of the journalists in Jakarta who had been covering the Bre-X story. They, unlike their peers outside Jakarta, had been able to spend time with the Bre-X executives and geologists, and had toured the Busang mine. Jay Solomon, a *Wall Street Journal* reporter who covered the Bre-X story, helped me out by steering me in the right direction. John McBeth at the *Far Eastern Economic Review* was one of the most knowledgeable and helpful. A seasoned reporter, McBeth was a New Zealander who had spent many years in Jakarta. He was on a first-name basis with all the businessmen and government officials who mattered. He was intimately familiar with the Bre-X story. McBeth proved to be a fountain of information, and what he didn't know he could learn by picking up the phone and calling one of his contacts.

McBeth was able to shed some light on who was in contention to purchase Bre-X. Both Barrick Gold and Placer Dome, two majors, were the leading contenders. The executives of both companies were in Jakarta for negotiations with Bre-X. The jockeying by Barrick and Placer Dome to buy Bre-X legitimized the company's claims. If these two majors were willing to throw money at Bre-X, certainly it must be the gold find of the century.

Let's not forget the charitable largesse that Bre-X bestowed on the local community. Bre-X had spent more than $1 million on a social development program for the indigenous tribes near Busang. It had built churches and schools and even organized sewing classes for the local women. Bre-X planned to open a fishery and poultry farming venture where the local tribes could raise and sell food to the mine. These contributions bought goodwill from supporters who wanted the venture to succeed. These advocates were also willing to quash any detractors of the project.

What were the red flags—waving in plain view—that everyone ignored?

Walsh, himself, for one. He had never had any success in mining; he had no track record at all. His personal bankruptcy and lack of success should have been considered.

How about the outrageous discovery numbers? From 70 million ounces to 200 million to 400 million, the numbers continued to climb. (To put this in perspective, the world's largest legitimate gold deposit had been discovered eight years earlier on another remote Indonesian island. That deposit contained 50 million ounces.) It was as if the Bre-X crowd could throw out any number that came to mind without the analysts and media questioning it.

The history of the Busang property showed little likelihood of gold. It had been explored by more than a dozen companies before Bre-X purchased it for $10,000. The other companies had found no gold and said the property was worthless. Why would anyone believe that Walsh, with no track record, would find what all the others never found?

There was the "accidental" fire at Busang in January that destroyed the building containing chief geologist de Guzman's geological map records. Then, just after the first independent verification of the gold was made, de Guzman mysteriously fell 600 feet from an enclosed helicopter to his death.

No one, *not one* of the Wall Street analysts who were telling their customers to buy the stock had actually seen gold at the site.

Finally, an independent mineral audit of the site revealed that only trace amounts of gold were found in the ground and there was "virtually no possibility of an economic gold deposit." The audit firm further revealed that the supposed gold deposit was "based on tampering and falsification without precedent in the history of mining."

Bre-X is similar to Enron, which in 2001 was the seventh largest company in America. There were literally hundreds of articles about Enron in publications from the *New York Times* to *BusinessWeek* to *Time* magazine—all about what a great company it was. *Fortune* magazine named Enron one of "American's Most Admired Companies" for six consecutive years. It all turned out to be a big scam. These scams are so ubiquitous, it seems like they're almost impossible to avoid.

The common element in both Enron and Bre-X, in hindsight of course, was the fact that it was not possible to verify the true business of either company.

Enron used a variety of accounting tricks to make it appear that it was more financially large and sound than it really was. Enron fooled a gullible media into hyping the company and it schmoozed Wall Street analysts to promote the company's stock.

With Bre-X, investment and mining professionals (as well as journalists) simply accepted the fact that there was gold under the ground. Gold, oil, and gas exploration are sectors in which scams are likely to occur because you can't really see the product. You are trusting someone to tell you the gold is really 20 feet below the surface, or the oil and gas is really thousands of feet below the surface. The investor can't independently verify the product's existence.

Does white-collar financial crime pay? You bet it does. When the Bre-X scam was exposed, Walsh took off for the Bahamas, where he lived in his luxurious home until he died in 1998 of an apparent aneurysm. He died before he could be prosecuted and had kept the millions that he made selling his stock at its height. As for John Felderhof, he gained $50 million from his stock sales and retired to the tropical and expensive Cayman Islands. A blundering sort of prosecution was brought against him in Canada, but his aggressive defense humiliated those authorities to defeat.

Felderhof was charged by the Canadian authorities at the Ontario Securities Commission with insider trading. No other officers, directors, or people associated with Busang were ever charged or arrested. The Canadian authorities acknowledged that they had no evidence that Felderhof was personally involved in the fraud. After prosecuting Felderhof over a seven-year period for insider trading, he was found innocent. It appears that the Canadian authorities, like the SEC in the United States, couldn't make a case against anyone involved in Bre-X. The fraud had happened in Indonesia and neither the Canadian nor U.S. authorities had any desire, ability, or experience to put together a case that emanated from overseas. So now Felderhof travels freely around the world, enjoying the fruits of his fraud.

Apparently, even death can't stop some financial serial killers. Michael de Guzman, supposedly dead from his helicopter fall, was recently reported to be alive and well, sipping cocktails in South America and enjoying the sun.

Postscript

After Bre-X collapsed, and investors lost billions of dollars, I, Tom Ajamie, went to the SEC's headquarters in Washington, D.C., to share all the facts from my investigation and to give them a road map on how to prosecute the Bre-X wrongdoers and some of the banks that I believed were complicit in the fraud. I was welcomed into a meeting room at the SEC where several SEC officials listened as I set forth the evidence. After I made a presentation over several hours, the leader of the SEC group told me that he would be in contact as the agency proceeded with its investigation.

I heard from the SEC only twice after that meeting. One of the agents called me to ask for the phone numbers of some of the Bre-X workers in Indonesia who might have some factual knowledge about the fraud. I told the SEC agent that he needed to travel to Indonesia to do his investigation; no one was going to talk to him by phone.

The second, and last, call I received from the SEC was from the same investigator. He complained to me that no one in Indonesia was taking his calls. He was surprised, but why should he have been? If you were involved in a fraud, and you lived on the other side of the world, would you return a call from some pencil pusher in Washington? Of course not. So the SEC's investigation (if it can even be called that) never gained ground, and the SEC never brought charges against any of the individuals involved.

Lessons & Takeaways

- There's a tremendous amount of work that goes into hyping a stock or something precious like gold. If you can learn to detect the hype, you can protect your savings from the financial serial killers who could be targeting you.
- In the case of Bre-X, the executives with the company took a worthless patch of land, marketed it to anyone that would listen, and used it to create a stock that was worth billions.
- Investors need to be careful of promotion and hype through investment newsletters. Who knows if they are "independent" by journalistic standards? Money could be exchanging hands to determine if a company is going to be included in these newsletters. Or, the newsletter writers could simply be old drinking buddies of the executives running the companies they claim to be covering without a bias. They portray themselves as independent newsletters providing exclusive, insider knowledge—while charging a steep price. Whether they are independent or not is the subject of debate. There is no industry monitoring of these newsletters, which number in the hundreds and cover risky investment areas such as oil, gas, and other commodities.
- Winning over the media is important to give the appearance of legitimacy in such a fraud. With the Internet and 24-hour business news coverage there are more ways for a fraud to reach you than ever before.
- Journalists earn their pay and reputation for "breaking news," for reporting stories and information before the competition. Even the most talented and conscientious reporter may get facts wrong and make mistakes. In other words, just because a reporter wrote a story about a company or financial transaction does not mean it is correct.

Lessons & Takeaways

- Do your own investigation into a company before investing in it. Don't rely on the media or stock analysts since they have their own agendas.
- Great investment opportunities are often kept quiet. By the time the average person hears about a wonderful opportunity, the easy money has probably already been made. Real opportunities or real ways to make money are treated like state secrets.
- There will be more gold mining frauds, so be on alert.

INTERLUDE

The Investment Industry Speaks

In these brief sections, veteran investment advisers and industry executives tell readers the tricks of the trade and what to watch out for in common transactions with a stockbroker or investment adviser.

Larry Papike, sixty-one, is an industry recruiter who looks for brokers and executives who want to leave one securities firm and join another. He has been involved in the securities business since 1978, where he started as a stockbroker.

There's one day Papike will never forget. He realized in early 1985 he would lose his business, a broker-dealer he had owned for four years, because a series of investments called private placements had blown up. A change in federal tax laws in 1986 killed a series of limited partnerships that were sold to investors as tax shelters. With that change in federal law, the investments became nearly worthless almost overnight. Investors lost money both on the investment, which was in real estate, and on a tax benefit they had already collected and had to pay back taxes. Papike has been wary of such high-stakes investments ever since.

When an investor meets an adviser, what he or she should look for is experience, Papike says. "Look for an adviser with a little bit of gray hair. If the adviser has been in the market for a short time, or is new in the business, they don't understand the down markets. A new adviser thinks that things just go up. He may put you into an investment thinking that it's a great product, the right product, but doesn't fully understand the risk."

Down markets test advisers and their abilities. "Until the adviser has to look clients in the eye and say, 'We've lost money,' that adviser doesn't understand the whole nature of the investment business, that markets go up and down."

You want to deal with an adviser who practices what they preach, Papike says. "You may meet a financial planner and talk about living trusts, but his record shows he has a tax lien. Ask them what they invest in, and if they don't own the product that they are recommending to you, run out the door."

If you are going for financial advice and financial planning, look for a certified financial planner, Papike says. "That doesn't mean that he's perfect, but it means that he's gone through the education and training and knowledge to do a plan for someone. If you're looking for planning, look for the CFP designation."

Pull the broker's records on the industry regulator's Web site. (See Chapter Fourteen to be walked through this process.)

The vast majority of people, 95 percent, don't bother to look at this information, he believes. "It will give you a great understanding of the adviser. It will show how many firms they've been with, the regulatory history, and if the adviser has had any problems with the law. It blows my mind the cavalier attitude people have when picking an adviser. They meet someone at a cocktail party and decide to invest with them."

When it comes to your money and your investments, don't be afraid to talk to the adviser about his or her money, he says. "How does this adviser get paid? People with big money, millions of dollars in assets, invest with a guy and don't know how he's getting paid."

Don't talk to your adviser about money just once, Papike says. It should be part of an ongoing conversation the client has with the adviser or broker. "Don't feel dumb or think it's awkward to ask your adviser about how he or she is making money. If you talk to an adviser in the very first meeting about how they're compensated, it does two things: it keeps the adviser on their toes, because they know the client is concerned about money and how it's spent. Everything is open and on the table so the adviser can't slip anything past you later. If he's aware that you are looking at how he's compensated and the cost, it certainly makes that adviser understand that you want to get a good deal. It's no different from buying a car."

Advisers can charge anywhere from fifty basis points—half of one percent—to 2.5 percent of the client's assets as a fee for his service. The client needs to be fully aware of that and must know the charges and how they compare against the market.

Demystify the process, and don't be intimidated because it involves money, Papike says. Shopping for an adviser should be like shopping for other services and products. "Don't go see one adviser. People are shortsighted when they're looking at this, and it's one of the most important decisions they can make in their life. It's like buying a car. You shop around and become an educated shopper."

The bottom line is people don't really understand finances, and no one wants others to find out how little they know. So people act as though they understand money, but they really don't. "You are talking about your money and future," Papike says. "If you pick a lousy broker, it can be your fault, especially if you didn't do the due diligence."

CHAPTER
FIVE

Stockbrokers, Greed, and Laziness

The business of retail securities firms like Merrill Lynch, with 16,000 brokers, and Morgan Stanley, with 18,000, is to sell consumers like you an array of financial products such as stocks, bonds, mutual funds, and variable annuities. Every time your money moves, every time you make a transaction and decide to buy, sell, or move assets around your account, the firm and the broker make money.

That's obvious, of course. A broker is not doing this service for free, nor should he. (Selling stocks has remained an overwhelmingly male-dominated business. A conservative estimate would peg 80 percent of the individuals licensed to sell securities in the United States as male. Therefore, we will stick to assigning brokers, and financial serial killers in general, a male pronoun.) They collect a commission on the transaction to sell the product, say selling 1,000 shares of Apple or IBM stock. Or, they can charge a yearly fee, equal to roughly one percent of the assets the client holds in that account.

> • ---
>
> Always make sure that your securities firm or investment adviser gives you an account statement, with an account number, which clearly shows what you own. Never give money to a so-called adviser who "comingles" client funds, meaning all money is put into one big pool. Financial serial killers like to siphon cash from such sloshed-together pools of investor money, and frauds and disasters can follow.
>
> --- •

There are 634,000 licensed securities brokers in the United States. Not all these people sell securities; a good number work as assistants to brokers or behind the scenes to keep business flowing. About half, 300,000, actually sell securities to clients and have a "book of business."

There are many upstanding, honest stockbrokers and investment advisers who help their clients figure out how to pay for retirement, their kids' college tuition, and manage the cost of long-term care in retirement. This book is not about those kinds of brokers.

It is a fact that some brokers and investment advisers—at some point in time—will put their own interests before those of the client. Brokers and executives who run broker-dealer firms can get greedy and lazy.

Clients can possess those qualities, too. It's part of human nature. Be on guard if a broker is trying to find your "get rich quick" button.

If just one percent of licensed securities professionals who sell products, say roughly 3,000 stockbrokers, are dishonest or unethical, even in the smallest degree, the public faces a risk that needs to be acknowledged and addressed. Keep in mind that the economic collapse of 2008 and 2009 directly affected the business of many stockbrokers, who suffered losses like their clients. How many of them have faced desperate financial situations that pushed them to look for new or alternative ways to make money?

Let's say that each of those ethically shaky 3,000 brokers has one hundred clients. That means 300,000 American consumers could be taking advice and handing over checks to a licensed securities person with questionable ethics. If those clients on average have $50,000 in an account, then $15 billion in hard-earned money, scraped together for retirement or college, could be at risk.

The retail securities business does not like to think of the risk of a dishonest or unethical broker in such a way. The risk, the securities industry says, is not pervasive, but rather isolated to specific individuals. The common wisdom among many executives in the retail securities business is that catching a broker who is a "bad apple" (in our terms, a financial serial killer) in the act of ripping off clients is virtually impossible.

When a reporter asks a typical executive from a retail brokerage firm how on earth could a broker get away with a scam that cost clients millions of dollars, so many executives have the same response it seems scripted. Wearing an expensive gray or navy blue suit, power cuff links gleaming, the executive casts a mournful look, glances down at the tassels on his Italian loafers, and says something like, *If a man is a thief, there is no stopping him. We want that thief out of the securities business as much as you do. If a broker is intent on stealing—and therefore harming—clients, he will find a way that will make it impossible to detect.*

In some instances, that is clearly the case. Some financial serial killers are too smart and sophisticated to be detected and caught. However, as we've shown, many financial serial killers use timeworn techniques, such as claiming a secret formula for investment success or returns each year of 15 to 20 percent, to nab prey. (As we will show in Chapter Eight, securities regulators routinely arrive late to a fraud or scam and don't act in time to protect investors.)

Common wisdom of the securities business can indirectly lead to the creation of a financial serial killer. One such notion is that star players, the golden boys, whether stockbrokers, investment bankers, hedge fund managers, whoever, are best off if they are left alone. The common mantra at many securities firms is: Do not bother the heavy hitter in the corner office! He knows what he's doing, he's making it rain, he's racking up the sales. He doesn't need someone from the compliance department bothering him with mundane questions about client account forms, expense reports, or trading documents.

One such heavy-hitting stockbroker, a true financial serial killer, who occupied the corner office at a national brokerage firm, was a wunderkind named Enrique Perusquia. His actions cost one client at least $68 million and he eventually pleaded guilty to securities fraud and was sentenced to six and a half years in federal prison.

Paine Webber Inc. recruited Perusquia from Lehman Brothers in 1994. When Perusquia joined his new firm, Paine Webber continued to allow him to operate his practice of buying and selling securities for wealthy investors by using offshore accounts. These accounts, set up in foreign countries, are legal as long as they are reported and taxes are paid. They are subject to abuse, however, when people use them to hide money from U.S. authorities in order to avoid taxes. Simply put, it was easier for Perusquia to manipulate these accounts because they were in foreign countries.

Now, in a post-9/11 world, federal law mandates that offshore financial transactions be more closely monitored. However, recent cases involving global banks show that firms are still going to great lengths to hide such transactions. That flies in the face of the effort to make brokerage firms scrutinize such offshore business much more closely. The culture that gives special privileges to star brokers still exists on Wall Street.

Perusquia apparently dictated to Paine Webber how he was going to manage part of his business, according to the Securities and Exchange Commission. "Specifically, as a condition of joining Paine Webber, Perusquia requested an account arrangement similar to the one that he had at his prior brokerage firm," the SEC said in a 2003 legal proceeding against Paine Webber. "Under that agreement, Perusquia arranged for certain of his clients [sic] to hold their funds in accounts at Swiss banks, and in the names of offshore companies that he helped establish. The Swiss banks then set up accounts at Paine Webber in the names of the Swiss banks (which were referred to as omnibus accounts)."

Perusquia was able to construct a complex maze of offshore accounts labeled with obscure names. This made the accounts impossible to identify, and they could not be linked to any particular individual or account holder. Anyone looking at the accounts would just see a name, but could not link this name to another account or to a particular person.

This confusing amalgam of accounts intimidated the prying eyes of Perusquia's supervisors or anyone else trying to oversee his activities. "Perusquia established sub-accounts at the Swiss banks in the names of offshore entities controlled by Paine Webber's clients. Perusquia conducted discretionary trades through the omnibus accounts, and then directed the Swiss banks to allocate the trades to specific sub-accounts on behalf of the various offshore entities," the SEC said.

A discretionary trade is one that the broker is allowed to make at his own discretion, without asking for permission in advance from his customer. Brokers will often advise clients to set up their accounts as discretionary accounts in order to give the broker the ability to make trades in the account without having to first get the permission of the customer. The discretionary account is especially attractive to customers who are very busy or those who are relying completely on their broker to make all investment decisions. There is nothing inherently wrong with a discretionary account; these accounts make complete sense for certain types of customers. They are, however, prone to abuse if they fall under the control of an unscrupulous broker.

Such complete discretion allowed Perusquia to get his hands on millions of dollars through theft or kickbacks, according to the SEC. "Perusquia's fraud involved investing large portions of his clients' funds in a small group of highly speculative gold mining firms while he simultaneously received secret payments from the mining companies, misappropriating money from the client accounts, and engaging in unauthorized margin trading."

Setting up a web of offshore accounts undoubtedly helped Perusquia's fraud work. He found and created a network of new investors to steal from, and abused his tried-and-true personal relationships that he had developed over the course of his life.

Enrique Perusquia conned everyone he came in contact with, from the people he grew up with as a child to the disabled land lady in Colorado who rented him a winter ski lodge. I, coauthor Tom Ajamie, came to know Perusquia well.

As with many frauds, Perusquia used family connections to nab his marks. Born in Mexico City to wealthy influential parents, Perusquia grew up among Mexico's elite. Perusquia's long-time family and social relationships evolved easily into business relationships, which he kept when he moved to New York to work in the financial industry.

As with many investment schemes, familiar and comfortable connections were a key element of the fraud. (See Chapter Eleven about affinity fraud.) These wealthy Mexicans were looking to diversify some of their savings outside their native Mexico and into the United States. Mexico has experienced several devaluations of its currency, whereas the United States has always been known as a stable monetary environment. These clients were also looking for someone in the United States they could trust. They did not want to give their money to a stranger.

Having grown up with Perusquia, they flocked to him. He shared their language, their cultural background, their circle of friends, and (they thought) their values. Here was someone just like them, but who lived in the United States and in its financial capital, New York—a city where many of them were lacking financial contacts.

Financial serial killers are known to exploit such seemingly benign traits as sharing a culture and common tongue to their advantage. A common language helps build trust. Many of the Mexican customers spoke English, but naturally they felt much more comfortable speaking Spanish.

Financial serial killers and predators like Perusquia are incredibly compulsive. Taking someone else's wealth is part of a financial serial killer's nature, and it was part of Perusquia's. He was compelled to ask for his victims' money, saying he would invest it, and that he could grow it. This included a disabled lady from whom he rented a ski home in Colorado. She needed every dollar of savings she had squirreled away in the bank. In his charming way, he assured her that he could invest her money, protect it, and make it grow. He talked her out of all her savings, which was about $200,000. He stripped her bare.

Perusquia even stole from an ex-wife. He'd divorced his third wife, Donna Bloomfield, and she got about a $1 million settlement, but she didn't know how to best invest the money. She did know that Perusquia could handle money successfully, at least according to him. He offered to invest her money for her.

The financial serial killer does not need to employ sophisticated tricks like those from a George Clooney heist film. Although he's a thief in an expensive suit, his techniques can be quite rudimentary and lack sophistication. Perusquia siphoned off money into his own personal account. He forged the client's signature to authorize moving that money around.

He used offshore accounts to help mask the fraud. As Perusquia moved money from account to account, it became more difficult to follow the money trail, which is exactly what Perusquia wanted. A casual review of the account activity would not have uncovered his fraud. He had made the transaction record so complex and convoluted that the services of a forensic accountant or investigator would have been needed to detect it. To unravel his complex web would have required days or weeks of work. The task would have been too daunting for the average compliance officer at a brokerage firm.

After I was first approached by some of Perusquia's customers, I took the same step I had taken in the Bre-X fraud case: I decided to hop a plane and meet the man who was alleged to have smoothly lifted the savings out of the hands of his customers. Within days of hearing the customers' plights, I was on a flight to San Francisco to hunt down Perusquia and hear his side of this unbelievable story of greed.

One of Perusquia's customers who hired me showed me account statements that he had received from Paine Webber. These statements clearly showed that the customer had $130 million in his account. Several days earlier the customer had received a phone call from the Paine Webber margin department. They told the customer that he actually owed the bank $2 million.

Upon learning this, I thought that there must be a simple and explainable mistake. If a customer has an account statement showing $130 million in the account, how could the client possibly owe $2 million? I was skeptical that the money had just disappeared. Perhaps Perusquia had mismanaged it. Maybe he had moved the money into another account. Most likely there was just a misunderstanding here. I decided to find Perusquia and have him explain this to me. Maybe Paine Webber had just made an error, or couldn't locate certain offshore accounts. I was confident that Perusquia would be able to clarify all this and make it right.

Before heading to San Francisco, I called Paine Webber to ask for Perusquia's address. No one had it. I thought it was odd that a major brokerage firm had lost track of its former star, but I had an old address for him, on Green Street, so I started there. When I arrived I saw a beautiful, tall high-rise overlooking the bay. It's one of the most exclusive residences in the city. The doorman told me that Perusquia had moved out of the building about a year earlier. He was living somewhere east of the city, supposedly in a neighborhood called Blackhawk.

I rented a car and headed east. About an hour later I was in the exclusive master-planned community known as Blackhawk. How to go about finding him now? I asked around at several restaurants and coffee bars for him. Finally someone told me that he lived in a gated community. I drove to the gated area and tried to get by security. They wouldn't let me pass. I made small talk with the guard and was able to get Perusquia's street address. I used that address and eventually found a phone number. I called and a woman answered. I asked for Enrique. She passed the phone to Perusquia. I explained that I represented some Paine Webber customers who had been told by Paine Webber that their accounts were missing money. I thought this was just a misunderstanding. Would he meet me now for a cup of coffee? He agreed.

Within thirty minutes I was facing Perusquia. Here he was, the Paine Webber heavy hitter. I had been told that Perusquia had generated more commissions for Paine Webber than any other broker. It was impossible to verify this, but the guy was truly a legend.

He was so powerful at Paine Webber's New York office that he dictated the terms by which he would work. For example, at one point he had tired of living in Manhattan. Perusquia had decided that the quiet and exclusive community of Stowe, Vermont, was more to his liking. He'd just jet into Manhattan to work from Monday through Thursday and then jet back home to Vermont on Thursday afternoon. There was no need for an apartment in Manhattan, since that would involve too much work to keep it up. Instead Perusquia rented the Presidential Suite at the Peninsula Hotel, where the hotel staff would attend to his every whim.

A true financial serial killer, Perusquia immediately tried to charm me and win my trust. Perusquia arrived at the coffee bar in a black Porsche Carrera, but he was careful to park it several blocks away so as not to attract too much attention. He then walked up to meet me.

"Hi Tom, nice to meet you," he said with enthusiasm, his voice brimming with cordiality. He was thin, handsome, and charming. He wore a silk shirt that was neatly tucked into his black trousers. His black leather loafers were freshly polished. His hair was trim and his complexion was smooth. He offered to buy me a cup of coffee and told me that I "looked like a runner."

Immediately Perusquia was doing what he did well: making a human connection. Offer a man a cup of coffee and find a common interest. In fact, I was a runner. So Perusquia and I immediately began talking about favorite runs, where they were and so on. High quality chitchat.

Perusquia then moved to religious backgrounds, hoping to score another common hit. Bingo! We were both raised Catholic. It was apparent that if Perusquia was accomplished at anything, it was conversation. He knew how to engage the other person, find a common link, and create a rapport.

We met over a period of two days. I could tell that he wanted me to trust him. He wanted to show that he was indeed authentic and honest. After that first meeting at the coffee bar, he took me to a Fresh Choice restaurant. This was a company he said he had raised money for—and one of the companies in which he'd invested his customers' money. When we walked into the restaurant, it seemed like just another salad bar. According to Perusquia, this was not just any salad bar. This one was special.

"Look Tom," he said, his voice proud. "Look at how clean this counter is. And look at how fresh the vegetables are. We put a lot of effort into making this a unique salad experience for our customers."

"We?" I thought. Who is "We?" Perusquia was an investor in this salad bar, but he was using *his customers'* money to make the investment. This wasn't his restaurant. He was buying its stock, or making a private investment of his customers' money in the company. None of the staff at the restaurant knew who he was. No one greeted him by name. He didn't venture into the kitchen where the vegetables were being sliced and diced and thrown into square plastic containers.

Perusquia took on the air of an owner. He wanted to make me feel as though I was with the guy who had created the company himself. He was trying to make me feel like an insider, someone who was a part of a company that was growing into something big.

The next stop that day with Perusquia was a large law firm that had a nearby office. Perusquia told me that the senior partners at this law firm would meet with him at any time because he was such a large investor in some of the law firm's clients. By that, he meant that his customers were large investors, but clearly he controlled their money. So he could just show up unannounced at this law firm and the senior lawyers would drop their pencils to meet with him.

It turned out just like that. We arrived at the law firm. Perusquia strode into the reception room and asked for one of the senior partners. The guy showed up and embraced Perusquia. Perusquia introduced me to the lawyer, then the two of them ducked into a conference room to talk privately about a large investment that Perusquia (meaning his customers) was making in one of the law firm's clients. If Perusquia's goal here was to show me he wielded some power at large law firms, he accomplished that.

• --

The financial serial killer will tout his exclusive connections to executives, lawyers and other insiders to create an aura of prestige.

-- •

Part of Perusquia's pitch to investors, and me, was the exclusive, inside knowledge he possessed of certain companies. Financial serial killers like to flaunt such connections, real or not. He said that he knew the management of some of the companies personally. That he could talk to management, that he was very connected, that he had the inside connections, that he had very high-level contacts—all this gave him a lot of credibility.

One of these companies was Shaman Pharmaceuticals. Lisa Conte, Shaman's CEO, would meet with Perusquia regularly. Perusquia invested some of his customers' money with this company, enough that he had Conte's private phone number. This was another one of "his" companies. He spoke like an owner, ticking off all the wonders of the company's natural drugs derived from plants in the Amazon. He spoke of their miraculous properties, how the ingredients had been used for centuries by the natives and could cure any disease.

Perusquia talked a lot, but he could never explain what happened to my client's money. After spending two days with him in his make-believe world, I had a sense that something was wrong. His cloying charm, as well as his grandiose persona and stories, raised far more questions than answers.

My legal team and I unraveled Perusquia's fraud over the course of several years. We spent millions of dollars and thousands of hours of time to unearth Perusquia's complex web of disguised accounts that spanned several countries from Europe to the Caribbean. We traveled, investigated, and sent legal subpoenas for documents to a variety of locations as we worked to piece together the fraud: Geneva, Vancouver, New York, Mexico City, and the British Virgin Islands, to name a few. We then organized our investigation files and handed them over to the SEC, the United States Attorney, and the FBI.

The SEC took this work, combined it with its own, and zeroed in on Perusquia's handiwork. "While at Paine Webber, Perusquia used large portions of the Paine Webber Omnibus Clients' funds to buy stocks and convertible bonds in three gold mining companies," the SEC said. "Perusquia accomplished many of the purchases by submitting to the Swiss banks letters that contained unauthorized cut-and-paste, or trace-over, signatures purporting to be client authorizations to transfer funds to buy securities."

In the end Perusquia was just a phony. He didn't own the restaurants, nor did he create the drugs. He had simply found companies that needed money, and he had given them his customers' savings. He had taken no risks himself. He was all too eager to put at risk the hard-earned money that his customers had entrusted to him. He had purchased, with other people's money, all the trappings of prestige: access to a large law firm, the private phone number of a CEO, as well as a Porsche and a home in a gated community. At his center, Perusquia was nothing but a con man with an insatiable thirst for the good life.

It appears that the only thing that Perusquia really did well was forge the signatures of his customers. He also fabricated phony account statements. Perusquia's forgery was too perfect, and that's what got him caught. My legal team and I obtained more than forty different documents with the client's signature on them. Then we photocopied the signature from each document onto clear plastic film. We then stacked each signature, one on top of the next. The forty signatures matched perfectly. This is humanly impossible. The only way for your signature to match perfectly each time you write it is to trace it. That is just what Perusquia had done.

That was Perusquia's undoing. We found the actual original signature of the customer that he had cut out and used as a template to trace his forgeries. This signature template, which Perusquia could easily slip into his wallet and carry at all times, allowed him to trace the client's signature at his convenience, effectively "authorizing" transfers to his personal accounts.

The forgery was so convincing that even the client whose signature Perusquia had stolen was tricked. We showed the client the signature on wire transfer documents. The client said, "Yes, that is my signature." It was actually Perusquia's trace of his signature.

Later, we asked the client, "Did you authorize all these transfers of your money to Perusquia's accounts?" The client responded, "Of course not. Why would I give away my money to my broker?"

That was the basis for the criminal charges against Perusquia— the theft of the money—and that's why he went to prison. If he had simply been a crummy stock picker, and put his clients' money into losing stocks, we probably wouldn't have had a very good case against him. There's no penalty for a broker choosing the wrong stock, but there are consequences to stealing money and forging signatures. The U.S. Attorney and the FBI took the results of our investigation into Perusquia's dealings and prosecuted him for theft. He later pleaded guilty and served his time in federal prison. I think we made our point.

Lessons & Takeaways

- Con artists work to control the conversation, talking fast, using exciting statements and acting like the victim's friend.
- The fact that a broker works for a large, national firm, with thousands of brokers occupying expensive offices, is no insurance that your broker is not a financial serial killer. Because Perusquia had first worked for Lehman Brothers, and then for Paine Webber, he appeared to be reputable on the surface. Simply put, there is not as much protection as you would think.
- In the securities business, a screening or compliance process can break down, and sometimes it happens with the firm's biggest, most important advisers. Perusquia received kickback checks sent to the office and no one caught on to him. He transferred money to his own account from the customer's account at the brokerage firm, and no one caught on.
- Star brokers, or heavy hitters, often are left alone with little supervision. They get special treatment. This can lead to disaster, like in the case of Perusquia.

CHAPTER
SIX

More Stockbrokers, Greed, and Laziness

Greed is a natural occurrence in each of us. We all covet something. The question is to what lengths we will go to get it.

Some stockbrokers certainly know how to identify the greed in investors' hearts and turn that into gold—for themselves. Financial serial killers push investors' emotional and psychological buttons and turn them into suckers, all because of the promise of easy riches.

Part of the history of the retail securities business is built on sales scripts and techniques to entice investors to commit to a stock and convince them to buy more, even if the investors want to get out.

One of the most notorious examples of the hard sell was the securities firm Stratton Oakmont of Long Island, an infamous brokerage synonymous with the phrase "boiler room" in the securities industry in the 1990s.

The firm was known for its rabid brokers selling ginned-up stock offerings that the firm's principals essentially created and controlled. The principals reaped huge profits when the brokers sold the stocks, often over the phone in an intense, almost abusive way, at times belittling clients into a sale.

Stratton Oakmont brokers essentially controlled the price of these stocks, first "pumping" them, or generating misleading trading activity, to a high price, and then "dumping" them on customers and selling valueless shares at a great profit.

The owners and principals of the firm made millions on the pump and dump, and many of the brokers who worked at Stratton Oakmont made hundreds of thousands. Some brokers made that in a single month of commissions by selling shares to investors whom they convinced that the price of the stock would only continue to skyrocket.

Many investors, of course, were wiped out when the false demand for the shares simply evaporated, and were left with shares of stock worth nothing.

Jordan Belfort was one of Stratton's founders, and he was convicted in 1999 of securities fraud. That means he made false or misleading statements, or omitted important information, in order to induce someone to buy a stock or a bond. He served about half of a four-year sentence. Later he wrote a book about being a thief in the stock market game, entitled *The Wolf of Wall Street*.

The book is a clear look into the sordid life of a financial serial killer.

"And what secret formula had Stratton discovered that allowed all these obscenely young kids to make such obscene amounts of money?" Belfort asks.

> For the most part, it was based on two simple truths: first, that a majority of the richest one percent of

Americans are closet degenerate gamblers, who can't withstand the temptation to keep rolling the dice again and again, even if they know the dice are loaded against them; and, second, that contrary to previous assumptions, young men and women who possess the collective social graces of a herd of sex-crazed water buffalo and have an intelligence quotient in the range of Forrest Gump on three hits of acid, can be taught to sound like Wall Street wizards, as long as you write every last word down for them and then keep drilling it into their heads again and again—every day, twice a day—for a year straight.

Yes, financial serial killers, as we've seen, prey upon the elderly and the poor. Those people are often desperate financially, and that means they are targets. A smooth-talking salesman also knows how to tickle even the most financially secure individual's greed, and that's what brokers at Stratton Oakmont often did.

As we have said before, some people running Ponzi schemes often don't have any intention of creating such a fraud. They simply begin taking money from one group of investors to pay the previous group, with the hopes of making it all back.

Similarly, if a broker worked at a place like Stratton Oakmont, and many others, he would run into intense moral challenges. When a customer buys or sells a financial product, the transaction must pass the "suitability" test. According to the SEC, that means that the broker must have a reasonable basis for believing that the recommendation is suitable for his client. In making that assessment, the broker must consider the investor's risk tolerance, other holdings of securities such as stocks and mutual funds, the client's income and net worth, financial needs, and investment goals.

The person selling you the product is also supposed to use due diligence to learn—which means to take the initiative—all the essential facts relating to you as a customer and investor. In other words, the stockbroker must ask, "Is this the right or suitable product to sell my customer?" Too often, Wall Street and stockbrokers eliminate that way of thinking, and look at clients as a group of people to whom they can sell not the best or most suitable products, but the most expensive products, or those most profitable for the broker and the firm.

Here is one ex-stockbroker's story about working at a notorious place of business, where selling Stratton Oakmont's inventory of weak stocks was the rule each day.

Now a photographer and family man, forty-something David K. believed he could make a career as a broker selling stocks— what he calls "ideas"—to clients in the early 1990s. Like many people who sell stocks, bonds, and mutual funds for a living, David did not have a background or advanced degree in finance. It's common for stockbrokers to take a circuitous route to the job, and to some extent David got his start with a love of fast cars and motorcycles.

A New Yorker and in his early twenties, David split up with a girl and ran all the way to California to put her far in his rearview mirror. He wound up selling Honda motorcycles a few blocks from the beach in Santa Monica. He called an office of Shearson Lehman Brothers and asked the manager what it took to be a broker. The response: You have to have a good voice, and you have to be good on the phone. The manager, who didn't mention a word about financial education or skills, wanted David to come in and meet with him.

That's when he got a bit of a break—soon after that phone call, a broker from Shearson Lehman walked into the Honda shop in Santa Monica. He was so impressed with David that he invited him to visit the firm the next day, and David was soon up and running as a trainee.

"I had a sales background," David says of his experience in the motorcycle business, "and I was always intrigued by what it meant to be a stockbroker. The stock market seemed like it was an exciting place."

He didn't start as a broker. It takes time and training to get a securities license. David started on the bottom rung of the ladder as a cold caller, and made five dollars an hour, up to twenty-nine hours a week. The broker he worked for was a couple of years older than David, and was making $200,000 per year. While David doesn't characterize his former colleague as a financial serial killer, the broker certainly knew how to "game the system," David says. The broker, an imposing six feet, six inches tall with a thick Brooklyn accent, spent time talking with his clients about how his investment choices had *not* performed. He commonly used phrases like "I never said that," or "I told you it was speculative," when on the phone to a client.

Another broker in that Shearson Lehman office, Bradley Ruderman, did wind up proving himself a true financial serial killer. Ruderman bounced around the brokerage industry throughout the nineties and wound up running "hedge funds" in Beverly Hills. He was sentenced to more than ten years in federal prison for cheating investors out of more than $25 million. He had the classic traits of a financial serial killer: he took from the people closest to him and promised fabulous returns. "Ruderman, forty-six, admitted bilking investors, many of them family members, out of millions of dollars by promising annual returns as high as 60 percent and sending fake account statements between 2003 and 2009," the Associated Press reported.

• ---

Some brokers are simply salesmen—if they weren't selling stocks they would be selling motorcycles, cars or electronics.

--- •

David's colleague, the Brooklyn dude built like a basketball player, was generous, and often picked up their lunch or drinks, David says. He also had a nice series of tricks to earn extra cash, such as buying stock at $10 per share and calling his clients and asking them to buy it for $10.25. Not only did he pocket the 25 cent spread on each transaction, he earned a commission.

The next level for David was to become an "account opener," which meant opening thirty accounts with minimum investments of $10,000 in order to become a stockbroker. It took him a little more than a year to get his securities license.

That was 1993, and David decided to move back to New York.

In New York, he joined a local firm where a family friend worked. Such connections are common in the securities industry, as they are in many industries. The big difference about the clubiness in the securities business is that it's practically the only industry where an employee such as a stockbroker and investor can agree to put the investor's life savings at risk, or "to work," as it is commonly phrased in the business.

A broker will often spend the first three to five years of his career developing a list of loyal clients—a "book of business" as it's known in the retail securities trade. The process of calling complete strangers on the phone or meeting them after work and convincing them to buy something as intangible as shares of stock can take its toll on both the caller and the listener.

"I was great at speaking with people, but the arduous task of cold calling and dealing with all the rejection was something I wasn't terribly crazy about," David says. The hard sell, essential to many kinds of securities transactions that do not involve financial planning, was tough. "I tended to empathize with the person on the other end of the line instead of just aggressively pushing past all their seemingly understandable objections to get them to acquiesce to my proposals."

David left that New York firm to join another local brokerage known for selling initial public offerings of biotech companies, a hot sector at the time, but his move was blocked because of deal-making on the corporate level. Employees from his old firm, where he had already resigned, were prohibited from joining the firm where he wanted to work.

David recalls that a friend of a friend knew a broker at Stratton Oakmont in Lake Success, New York. In the spring of 1994, he was twenty-six and living in New York City. David had earned a license to sell stocks and bonds, and although he wanted to make riches, he also wanted to do the right thing by his clients. (An old saying for brokers in the securities business is based on hanging on to clients: "Have 100 clients and do right by them for years, and you'll live like a king.")

"When a client said, 'No, I don't have the money,' I tended to believe them or take them at face value," David says. "The typical broker would not hear 'no,' but they would hear that as 'not saying yes yet.' It's an aggressive mind-set."

David believed, perhaps naively, that he would offer "ideas"—meaning stocks—in as compelling a manner that he could, so clients would naturally want to do business with him, and not need to be coerced. "They would see that I was a good guy with something great to offer."

With that belief, he walked into Stratton Oakmont. Over the next few months he worked there, he saw staggering levels of personal excess by the brokers, all due to the wealth they created for themselves by hitting upon and taking advantage of people's need, desperation, and, in many cases, greed.

The firm was set in a huge sprawling business park on Long Island, and David, the former motorcycle salesman, recalls the parking lot with a painful relish: "I rode in from the city with my friend, who had a Chevy Chevette, a cheap car with a hatchback."

It was probably the grungiest car in the lot, he says. "The principals and the big brokers all had the top-of-the-line cars: Rolls Royces, Bentleys, Ferraris, Lamborghinis. They were all wild colors, and these were guys in their early twenties to early thirties."

The inside of Stratton Oakmont was impressive, too. "The main room was 30,000 square feet, and had rows of desks, as if it was school, with everybody facing the windows. It looked like it was the size of a football field, full of brokers."

The back half of the room was where cold callers, like David, stood all day long and generated leads they handed to brokers at the front of the room. Some of the cold callers were working for specific brokers. The target was to find investors with at least $100,000 already invested in the stock market; they had to have a history of purchasing stocks and be open to sales pitches on stocks, or "ideas," to invest.

The leads came from the credit reports of small business owners.

Cold callers like David didn't sell. They asked the prospective client for the opportunity to send out a business card and information about the firm. "We would say, 'Please allow this broker who I work for, who is terrific, to give you a call in the future and present an idea to you,'" David recounts.

The goal was to "qualify" the person, something prohibited in the securities business today. "We were looking for stock people who would buy over the phone and look to make a $10,000 investment on the first investment," he says.

David had his securities license from the National Association of Securities Dealers, now FINRA—more on that organization later—when he arrived at Stratton Oakmont. Management wanted him to go through their training before he could go it alone.

"The greed was amazing. At the end of the month, they would have meetings and ask individual brokers how they did. This was to stoke the rest of the room, and get those other brokers motivated. This guy just started out on his own, and he just made $150,000 in commission, all by himself. The intention was to plant that seed in the other brokers' minds, to show them that this was possible. The house takes half, so the payout to that broker is $75,000, before taxes, but you're thinking, *he's just beginning*."

The opportunity to make that much money impressed David. "I was making enough money to pay my rent and have some money in my pocket, but I was not getting rich by any stretch of the imagination. I was amazed by what was happening, and the characters this was creating. There was machismo, and the mindset was, with my money I was going to buy my Ferrari tomorrow, or take a private helicopter to Atlantic City."

"It was a little disgusting to witness, and there were some people who had moral issues with what they were doing. People were using drugs, cocaine to stay up and work, and for some to blot out the voices in their head."

Over the phone, David attempted to start the relationship by offering something familiar and benign sounding. Dr Pepper was the stock he pushed. He had helped sell it when he was a broker in training at Shearson Lehman—the firm was an underwriter, meaning it brought to the public shares of companies who want to raise capital from the public markets.

David put his knowledge of Dr Pepper to use at Stratton Oakmont. After it went public, one persistent market rumor was that another company would attempt to buy out Dr Pepper. When a company becomes an acquisition target, its stock price often can take off.

"Let's get the relationship started by you buying Dr Pepper, which we believe will be taken over," he would say. He called clients with the Dr Pepper takeover idea, priming them for a more far-out-sounding IPO. "The takeover idea has urgency built right into it." Greed and urgency are a powerful combination.

He would tell clients: "I don't know if it's going to happen today. It *could* happen today. It *could* happen tomorrow. Mr. Jones, get involved with me *now*, because once you read about it already happening you've missed the opportunity."

Then, he would point out other stocks that had been taken over and seen their values shoot up. "You're trying to build the urgency. It's a pretty simple idea to sell, as opposed to, 'I just like the earnings growth.' With that, there's no urgency there to build" into selling the client.

David used the Dr Pepper takeover idea to get the clients on the books. Opening an account means getting personal information, including social security numbers. That meant he could try to sell Stratton Oakmont IPOs to them later.

Once the check came in to pay for that initial investment in Dr Pepper, he was back on the phone that very day, "showing him one of *our* ideas. And one of *our* ideas, or one of Stratton Oakmont's ideas, was one of the stocks they underwrote, which they made a market in."

"I had success in conveying the urgency of Dr Pepper," David says. "We were raising money on it. This is what I'd typically say:

"Mr. Jones, there's all these signs on the wall. This is what the New York Times *said about Dr Pepper. This is what the* Wall Street Journal *said about Dr Pepper."*

"I just don't have the money," the client might respond.

"I understand that. But if I were to show you a Wall Street Journal *article that will appear one month from now, and Dr Pepper, which is trading right now at $20 per share, one month from now is trading at $40 per share, would you have wished you had taken a position here today?"*

"Yes, of course."

"So do this: Since you can't work with me on the original order of 10,000 shares, work with me small. Just get started. Judge me on my price and timing. If I'm right, next time, you'll work with me bigger and better."

"The broker is constantly saying things like that," David says. "And if you were right, and Dr Pepper did get taken over, you look like a genius and the client is waiting there with bated breath."

At Stratton Oakmont, there was a fever pitch to the entire experience in order to keep this momentum going, he says. "There wasn't a lull. No one ever said, Hey, the market's down. It didn't matter what the market was doing. This was a sales force. This wasn't a thinking room. No one was coming up with strategies or seeking to find the next best idea. Ideas (again, meaning stocks) like Dr Pepper came about from time to time, but the real focus was on the Stratton Oakmont initial public offerings." Some of the IPOs, Steve Madden Ltd. and KICK (the stock symbol for Master Glazier's Karate International Inc.), are reminders of a time when people believed investing in shoe companies and karate schools could lead to fabulous riches.

"The watches, the clothes, the stories, all seemed very sexy," he says. "But the price I'd have to pay to get that . . . Once I was there for a little while, it was a process for me to observe this, and it amazed me."

The day-to-day routine was for the brokers to fight to stand out and gain attention. "I saw this one team, a pair of guys, get on the phone and say, 'Mr. Jones, if you work with me on this, you buy 250,000 shares at $3 per share.' They just asked for $750,000, an ungodly amount of money. In an effort to show the person that you have the balls to deal with that type of money, and to show it's a good amount, the broker went dead silent. Some customers would hang up, but if the client's response was, 'That's just too much money for me,' from the sales standpoint, that's great. You're on the way to winning. The client didn't say no to the idea, he's saying the size or amount is too much. So, you keep pushing him on the size."

"I had limited success there," David says. "What's wrong with me? I showed up with a conscience."

There were some brokers who would only deal with the big accounts, $250,000 and up, and they'd let the account openers— small fry like David—take all the rest. They would implore David to "land me the whale, bring me the whale."

When a whale was on the line, "A crowd would form around the broker, a mass of guys, with the hair slicked back and everyone wearing the suits, when the broker was closing the big client, he'd hit speakerphone, and the entire room would have to be dead quiet, or the client would hear them." It was calm and silent in the massive room, the dozens of brokers waiting to hear the client say yes. "It was a lot like being in high school, and you turn the corner of the hall and there's a fight going on and everyone would be dead silent because if you made noise it would attract some authority and the fight would be broken up. The thought that went through my mind was, This is nuts! It's crazy! The wealth that's being generated here!"

Using such high-pressure sales techniques that showed clients no regard or respect weighed on David and his buddy with the hatchback. "We were not cut out for this existence. It always seemed to be the guy who was the dishwasher or the used-car salesman who was thriving."

Working at Stratton Oakmont had its thrills, especially for a young man who loved fast cars and motorcycles. "It was like going to an exotic car show on the way to work. So that was exciting, but you knew there was something wrong about it. It was akin to the *Wizard of Oz*, and it didn't take long to see there was someone behind that curtain."

Stratton Oakmont not only made a market in stocks but also had an inventory in those stocks. Some companies appeared legitimate, David says, but the original deals, the private placements and the bridge loans, were held by Stratton insiders.

"And that's where people really got rich. If you did a private placement with Stratton Oakmont, once the shares were converted and went through the IPO process, those private placement shares became seriously inflated."

That's when the brokers focused on the clients' greed, David says. "On the day that the stock went public, you would say to someone, Mr. Jones, you've been a client of mine for a while, and I'll get you some shares of the IPO—*if I can*—but I'm going to have a much better chance of getting you a thousand shares at $4 per share if you commit to buying 10,000 more on the open market."

That part of the commitment could cost the client as much as $20 per share. That's how the brokers zeroed in on the client's greed, and sometimes got him in deeper than he ever imagined. The brokers, who controlled the supply of the stocks, cleaned up in commissions. The owners of Stratton Oakmont, who essentially owned the product, became extremely wealthy. The supply of IPO stock was tight and the demand far exceeded the turnover, David says. Typically, the big sellers often were insiders in the company.

When David graduated from account opener to broker on the floor of Stratton Oakmont, the end of his time at the firm was near. The firm didn't want him to sell clients' stock, even though it had doubled or tripled in value and the client was clamoring to cash out and take profits. If most customers are holding their stock, and won't sell it, then fewer shares are available for sale; the fewer the shares available, the easier it is to drive up their price. "You actually had to fight someone to sell your clients' stock," he says.

"Any time the broker wanted to sell stock, it wasn't so easy," he explains. "It was not a rubber stamp or a signature and then being told, take it to the traders and they'll sell it for you. Management gave you a sort of implied guilt trip. They'd say things like, 'You're not helping the cause by letting this person sell.'"

"I left Stratton when they basically told me, 'Your clients are not allowed to sell.' I said to myself, *This is wrong. I've learned about this client. I can't do this.* At the end, I was both an account opener and on my own stage. It was ridiculous. I had to battle someone to get the approval to sell something. If the client just bought at $7 per share, and now it's $13, and he wants to sell but can't, then what am I here for? It made no sense. It just wasn't worth it."

He says he never hurt a client of his own there. However, when he handed off leads to another broker, he did not know whether that person got fleeced or not.

FINRA finally decided enough was enough and kicked Statton Oakmont out of the securities business in December 1996. The firm no longer exists, but many of the brokers who worked there are currently working at other brokerage firms around the country.

FINRA barred Stratton Oakmont's two founders, Jordan Belfort and Danny Porush, from the securities business.

Belfort spent almost two years in jail for running a pump-and-dump stock scheme that hurt investors with losses of close to $200 million. Leonardo DiCaprio is reportedly going to star in the film version of his life story, with Martin Scorsese directing. He is now a motivational speaker. Danny Porush pleaded guilty to money laundering and securities fraud in 1999 and served 39 months in prison. In 2008, *Forbes* reported he was driving a Bentley and living in a house by the Woodfield Country Club in Boca Raton, Florida.

After leaving Stratton Oakmont in the fall of 1994, David moved to a brokerage based in midtown Manhattan, Duke & Co. He went back to opening accounts selling clients Dr Pepper, because it hadn't been taken over.

He had learned from his experience at Stratton. "I was going to take advantage of Duke. They were bringing a company public, an IPO called Renaissance-FAIR. It was an IPO for outdoor fairs where people call waitresses 'wench' and drank 'grog,' not beer. This is what I was encouraging people to buy."

He put the experience from Stratton Oakmont to use to sell for Duke & Co., and he had conversations that sounded like this:

"Mr. Jones, my prior company participated in an IPO for a company called Octagon. It came out at $4 per share and went to $20 per share. My clients have bought 10,000 shares. That means my clients made $160,000. Mr. Jones, if I did that for you, would you love me?"

"Yes, I would."

"Good, now when you open your accounts, do you do that individually or joint?"

He went immediately for the jugular, his confidence at an all-time high. He quickly opened twenty accounts, and asked them to buy Dr Pepper and get them on the firm's books.

"When Renaissance went public, there was a celebration at the Oak Room in the Plaza Hotel," David says. "I generated $40,000 in commissions, so I earned $20,000 for that single day, after three months' work. I was making a few thousand dollars a month opening accounts. But that day was my best in the business.

"The guy sitting next to me at the Oak Room made half a million dollars, and so I sat there and felt like a loser, even though I'd just made twenty grand. I thought, How could I have done better?

"The stock, Renaissance, went from $7 per share to $13 per share. I changed firms again, and I encouraged the clients who came with me to dump the stock."

• ---

Stockbrokers—and indeed, many salespeople in general—try to imbed urgency into their conversations with clients. In fact, brokers often point to news stories to buttress their hard-sell techniques. It's part of creating a "story" around a company or stock.

--- •

Remember, when it comes to buying stocks, the investment pros use "fundamental" information about a company—basic financial information such as earnings or how much debt it has on its books. When investing, fundamentals are much more important than a story. Stocks with a great story can fail when the story simply comes to an end—say when it turns out that not many people want to spend weekends with their families at a Renaissance fair. Stocks with proven earnings growth and manageable debt usually will retain some sort of value.

People sit around and think about their money, dwelling on it, worrying about it, and that's when they can be vulnerable to cold callers or introductions to stockbrokers whose ethics are weak or simply lacking.

Deciding what to do with money can cause an incredible amount of stress. People may lack money to pay bills and could be desperate. Or, did they just come into an inheritance and are trying to figure out what to do with it? Do they need more money for their daughter's college tuition? Clients must be aware of their vulnerability and understand that they, or a loved one like an elderly parent, can turn into a victim.

At the same time, it's not socially correct to talk about money or discuss their own investments, David says. "What I've found is that a lot of people are alone with these thoughts. Many people don't feel that they have enough money, and because they're leading lives with responsibilities and obligations, they need more. Will I be able to pay the college tuition? The medical bills? Will I be able to pay insurance on my real estate? Am I living too far above my means?

"So, if someone calls you up, and says, 'Mr. Jones, I just made a client 30 percent on his money in one month, and I've got another idea, and I think I can make you 100 percent on your money,' I guess, sanity and responsibility may take a very quick backseat to greed and desire."

(Brokers and advisers still cold call to find new clients, but rules and regulations have somewhat limited their reach.)

Investors sometimes fall in love with losing stocks. "Investment psychology is funny. People don't like being asked, 'Do you have a plan for when things go wrong?' A lot of times, people will tend to keep a losing stock in a portfolio, because selling it means that they have to face themselves and say, '*I've made a mistake.*'"

Over time, David's approach to investing became more intelligent as he learned more about the market and employed sophisticated strategies that locked in gains and hedged against losses.

"My approach was to attempt to create urgency. I wanted to present a game plan to how I invested. At certain times, you play offense, buy stocks, and let them run. And there were certain times to take profits, and hedge and short the market altogether." He stopped selling securities to clients in the fall of 2009, after sixteen years in the business. "I didn't have a lot of clients, but my clients stuck with me, because I did right by them."

Not all people are cut from the same cloth, and there are people who will say yes to a voice over the phone, David says. "I didn't work well like that, and that's why I think I ultimately didn't succeed in the business to the level that many people did."

"There are impulse buyers, gamblers, who are looking for this type of opportunity. One person I did speak to was Sherwood Schwartz, the producer of *Gilligan's Island*, the *Brady Bunch*, and others. I had just happened to call when his people, his line of defense, wasn't around. A very nice guy. And evidently, on Wall Street, he had a reputation of opening a lot of accounts and liking the action."

"When I called him back, his people blocked me from him and promptly said I shouldn't call him again. I was someone who had gotten through who was not supposed to get through."

The Shearson Lehman Brothers way was very direct, David says. If a broker had a little bit of the customer's money, he had their attention. Now, his job was to go out and get a lot more of their money.

In fact, the firm had a rebuttal book to help train young brokers like David. It was filled with responses and lines for brokers to engage clients and sell them products over the phone.

It was all scripted, he says. "I'm sure it sounded like I was reading, but it worked. It was almost as if the person wanted to hear this. Their sense of greed overpowered reason." This was all before the wide use of the Internet, so there was no Google search or other databases to use and easily check out the backgrounds and histories of brokers and advisers.

With relish, David recalls a few of the scenarios:

"Mr. Jones, we have new and interesting products. Send me a copy of your portfolio, and I'll have it analyzed by my department."

"Mr. Jones, I'm asking you to buy $2,500 worth of stock. After commission, after the government, I can't even buy myself lunch. This isn't about the money. This is about me being right."

"Fine, Mr. Jones. Just buy one share. I don't care. Just work with me on the pricing and timing of the stock."

Sometimes, David opened an account and the person at the other end of the line would apologize because it wasn't a bigger account. Or, they might mention that they had a bank CD coming due and could invest in six weeks. *"Mr. Jones, the idea isn't going to be here in six weeks. Get started with me right now."*

"Mr. Jones, are you wearing a skirt? Do you have any balls? You have to ask your wife if you're going to buy a stock? I'll give my mom a call and ask her if I can sell it to you."

The stockbroker can be bigger than life, David says. If he wants to appear that way, he sure won't tell you he took the subway to meet you. A broker can sweep someone off their feet with a velvety voice.

Yes, even the timbre of voice can be extremely important. One broker at Stratton Oakmont had a knack of turning his voice into a woman's, so it would appear to be his secretary calling the client.

Lessons & Takeaways

- Who's gaining from the transaction you are about to enter into? Is it you or some financial institution?
- Have you asked how the transaction works? Exactly how much are you paying here? Does the answer make sense?
- Why do you have to make the transaction right away, especially if you are interested in protecting your savings or increasing the amount of your money over the long term?
- Should you invest if you feel like your arm is being twisted, or should you walk away?
- Are you aware of your own greed or your own shortcomings when it comes to investing?
- Beware of commodities and leverage, or borrowing to pay for securities transactions.
- Securities firms are not allowed to use the word "guarantee" about stocks.
- Keep calm. The market is going to be open every day. Know who you are. So if a broker calls you and says, "If you don't do this right now, you're going to miss it," be willing to miss it.
- Slow down. If you find a broker or adviser, look them up on the Internet (see Chapter Fourteen) before investing.
- Remember the broker is part of a wider corporate culture. If he's not selling product, management simply could stop saying hello to him.
- The investor can't be lazy. Is making eight percent and not understanding how it's done worth more than making four percent and understanding the process?

- Stratton Oakmont and Duke—the names sound more like country clubs than real businesses. Firms at times want to appear to be something that they are not. Ask about the name. Is there a real Mr. Stratton or Mr. Oakmont. Is there really a Mr. Duke somewhere?

CHAPTER
SEVEN

Hedge Funds and Private Placements: Cachet and Exclusivity Can Cost You

For all the risks and pitfalls we've described, the stock market has many benefits. First, it's a public marketplace. Publicly traded shares of companies in the United States are either listed on an exchange, or traded in the over-the-counter marketplace.

Public companies need to file a tremendous amount of information with the SEC, which was created in 1934 during the Great Depression to enforce federal securities laws and regulate the securities industry.

From an investor's standpoint, that's clearly positive, because investors rely on public information about companies (e.g., earnings and debt) to decide whether to buy or sell shares.

Private investment vehicles for the rich, specifically high-end hedge funds and their bastard cousins, private placements, play by a different set of rules. We will tell you how.

Late in 2009, a hedge fund scandal erupted on Wall Street and into the corporate offices of some of the best-known companies in the United States.

The list of individuals who allegedly passed along confidential insider information reads like a Who's Who of the top tiers of corporate America: senior executives at IBM, Intel, and Advanced Micro Devices, a top lawyer at a prestigious Boston law firm, a trader at a Bear Stearns hedge fund, and a consultant at McKinsey & Co., a firm that offers business consulting services to the largest corporations in the country.

If government charges are proven to be true, this dragnet will have caught some of the most powerful people in the business world passing along confidential inside information in violation of the law. Individual investors cannot compete against those elite investors who have access to high level confidential information— insiders who will earn profits that others have no opportunity to ever enjoy.

We begin with a short explanation of hedge funds, one of the most misunderstood private investment vehicles on the market.

A hedge fund is an investment fund that is available to sophisticated investors who meet certain financial standards that qualify them to invest in these types of funds. Hedge funds are typically only available to professional or wealthy investors, although recently some of those rules have been removed or relaxed.

Hedge funds are supposed to be offered solely to what are known as "accredited investors." An accredited investor is an individual with a minimum net worth of $1 million or a minimum income of $200,000 in each of the last two years, and a reasonable expectation of keeping that income level in subsequent years.

Hedge funds are generally unregulated—*they are not required to give information to the SEC and are not subjected to review by the regulators*. Hedge funds are exempt from the same rules and regulations governing mutual funds. Hedge funds aren't even required to keep audited books and records.

Hedge funds can engage in a wide range of investments and trading activities that are not normally engaged in by mutual funds. Each hedge fund has its own investment strategy that determines the types of investments it will make.

Investors in hedge funds are required to be sophisticated. The idea here is that sophisticated investors are more likely to understand the risks involved in hedge funds, and are able to withstand potential large losses.

The fees are high. (Perhaps wealthy investors feel that if they are paying more, they are getting a better, more elite and exclusive service.) A hedge fund manager is paid both a management fee and a performance fee, which is sometimes called an incentive fee. Management fees typically range from one percent to four percent per year of total assets under management, with two percent being the standard amount.

Performance fees are calculated as a percentage of the funds' profits. A typical hedge fund manager receives a 20 percent performance fee from the funds' profits. The purpose of these fees is to incentivize the fund manager to generate returns by allowing the manager to share a percentage of the returns that are earned.

There are several criticisms of performance fees in hedge funds. One is that the performance fees incentivize the hedge fund manager to take a higher degree of risk because he is being paid a percentage of profits.

Hedge fund managers normally do not share in losses; if the fund does not make money, or loses money, the hedge fund manager will not receive a performance fee. But the hedge fund manager does not have to pay money back to the fund if he has a poor year and the investor loses money that year. So while the hedge fund manager takes a share of the profit, there is no mechanism for him to share losses.

Hedge funds will typically use leverage, meaning they will borrow money in order to make investments. Leverage can increase profits, but also increase losses. Some hedge funds borrow amounts that are many times greater than the principal amount invested in them. It is not uncommon for a hedge fund to borrow $9 for every $1 received from its investors.

An inherent problem with this practice is a loss of only 10 percent in value of the investment in the hedge fund will wipe out 100 percent of the value of the investor's stake. This is equivalent to a homeowner buying a $100,000 home by putting down $10,000 in cash and taking out a mortgage for the remaining $90,000. If the value of the home declines by a mere 10 percent, which is something that many homeowners have experienced over the past few years, then the homeowner's entire cash investment in the home has been wiped out.

Some hedge funds have been known to leverage themselves to ratios as high as 20:1 or 30:1. Thus, even a small market loss can lead to catastrophic damage and steep losses to the fund.

Hedge fund managers seem to have a higher appetite for risk, as do their investors. Hedge funds are more likely than other types of funds to take on risky investments such as subprime mortgages, high-yield bonds, and distressed securities.

These funds also often lack transparency. The managers of hedge funds normally apply their own proprietary trading models, which are kept secret. They do not want competitors at other hedge funds to know anything about the computerized trading models they are using. Thus, the means by which they make their money are shrouded and it can be difficult to know the inner workings of the funds or how the managers are generating their returns. Investors normally do not know the trading strategies used by the hedge fund, and often they cannot find out if the investments are diversified or if an investment manager is using large amounts of borrowed money.

A typical public investment fund, such as a mutual fund, is required to be registered with the SEC. Hedge funds are not required to be registered with the SEC and thus are able to avoid these regulations because of certain exceptions in the laws.

As private and unregulated entities, hedge funds are not required to disclose their activities to regulators or other outside parties. This is in contrast to mutual funds, which normally have to meet certain regulatory requirements and disclose their activities and investments.

Stay away from hedge funds unless you are very wealthy and financially sophisticated.

Recently the SEC began investigating possible insider trading by hedge funds.

Hedge funds seem to have captured the popular imagination in recent years, and many investors have flocked to them. Stories of fabulous riches, like certain hedge fund managers earning over $1 billion per year, have propelled these funds onto the cover of magazines and their managers onto various "highest earners" lists. The aura of exclusivity and privilege projected by hedge funds has increased the clamor of people who are racing to invest their money in these seemingly magical investment vehicles.

Yet not much is known about the shadowy world of hedge funds.

For years rumors of insider trading by a number of hedge funds have swirled around them. Insider trading is the illegal trading of securities by people who have access to "material nonpublic information."

Material nonpublic information is the type of knowledge that might affect the stock price or influence investors' decisions. One example of material nonpublic information would be any information about a company's earnings that had not yet been released to the public. If the earnings, when announced, are better than had been expected then the price of the stock will likely move up. If the earnings are worse than had been expected, then the stock price will likely fall. You can see why an investor who has advance notice of a company's earnings before everyone else would have an advantage over other investors.

This type of trading is prohibited by law since it gives investors with the insider information an unfair advantage over other investors who do not have access to this information. To level the playing field, Congress, regulators, and the courts have tried to create a system that gives all investors access to the same information and does not advantage those who have insider contacts.

Toward the end of 2009 the government made its most high-profile series of arrests ever of hedge fund employees for allegedly trading stocks based on access to illegal insider information.

Armed with confidential informants, wiretaps, and software tools, the government charged twenty money managers, lawyers, and others investors with illegal insider trading, and several have already pleaded guilty.

The largest fish caught in this net was Raj Rajaratnam, the billionaire manager of the $7 billion Galleon hedge fund. Rajaratnam made his billions, and placed himself among the richest people in the United States, through trading in his Galleon fund. There is no doubt now that the government prosecutors believe that illegal insider trading is endemic at certain hedge funds.

Prosecutors have already obtained guilty pleas from a network of hedge fund managers in Massachusetts and California, including a guilty plea from a key conspirator to the alleged insider-trading ring at Galleon, Roomy Khan. For many years Khan had worked for Intel and had faxed confidential information about Intel's chip orders and selling prices to computer makers to someone at Galleon.

Khan eventually quit Intel and then went to work for Galleon. She was later fired from Galleon for violating company policies by trading securities in her own account on the side. Prosecutors allege that even after Khan left Galleon, she continued to feed insider information to Galleon about companies such as Google, Polycom, and Hilton.

Meanwhile, Rajaratnam has been charged with running an insider-trading scheme from Galleon that benefited the hedge fund to the tune of millions of dollars. The Justice Department charged Rajaratnam and others with cultivating and relying on a vast network of company insiders and consultants to procure this illegal insider information. Some of these inside tips included advanced information about the earnings of IBM, Advanced Micro

Devices, and Lenovo Group. A former senior vice president at IBM has already pleaded guilty to providing insider information about Sun Microsystems.

Loaded with this advance information, an investor can reap millions in profits by buying the stock of a company before other investors hear the news that earnings will be better than expected, or avoid losing millions of dollars by selling a stock in advance of the public hearing that the company's earnings will be worse than was expected.

Are some hedge fund managers financial serial killers? If the federal allegations against Galleon and its network of partners prove to be true, we would say, in this case, yes.

Hedge funds like Galleon are associated with elite deal-making on Wall Street. Far from the glass and granite canyons of lower Manhattan, brokers to wealthy investors in the Midwest or Southeast pitch exclusive deals that promise high risk and high returns.

There's another type of investment ensnaring investors, called private placements. Not a hedge fund, private placements are stocks, bonds, or other instruments, often promissory notes, sold to investors by companies but not traded on the public markets.

The number of deals is growing and private placements are now beginning to come under increased scrutiny from regulators. The collapse of two such deals over the summer of 2009 shed light on the seedy process by which many securities firms bring these deals to market and sell them through their advisers and brokers to the public.

Many are questioning the due diligence performed on private placements, along with the due diligence fees broker-dealers earn when they sell the deals. To industry insiders, they are known as "Reg D" offerings, because of how they are filed with the SEC.

The two terms—Reg D and private placements—are used interchangeably.

"Reg D offerings receive virtually no regulatory pre-screening at any level of government," Denise Voigt Crawford, Texas Securities Commissioner and President of the North American Securities Administrators Association Inc., said in a September 2009 speech in Denver at a meeting of state regulators. "As a result of shortsighted state law pre-emption, investors have been exposed to far more risk in private placement offerings than Congress likely could have imagined," she said.

Because they are so poorly vetted, private placements are "a national debacle," says Brian Kovack, president of Kovack Securities Inc., a small securities firm in South Florida.

When the SEC created Reg D offerings in 1982, the intention was to simplify capital-raising for small-business owners. Reg D contains exemptions from federal registration for limited offerings of securities. The goal was to cut some of the red tape of filing with the SEC, thus helping the little guy get his hands on capital to grow his business.

Intended as a helping hand to small business owners, Reg D has turned into a thriving, legitimate way for financial serial killers to operate. The types of Reg D offerings and private placements are all over the map, and they have had a history of problems. Brokerage executives still recall with dread the disastrous Prudential Securities private placements. In the late 1980s, more than 100,000 investors put $1.4 billion into Prudential limited partnerships that wound up being worth almost nothing.

Reg D offerings aren't the small potatoes that the SEC had in mind back in 1982.

These funds are so poorly regulated that securities firms often leave the actual analysis of the offerings to outside, third-party due-diligence firms *who are paid by the firm issuing the private placement* for their report. Those shops typically consist of attorneys who are paid by the issuer to write a report that evaluates the viability of the issuer's deal. The due-diligence firms typically receive fees ranging from $6,500 for small offerings to $50,000 for complex deals, say brokerage executives familiar with the arrangements.

In addition to a possible conflict arising from receiving fees from the companies they analyze, due-diligence firms often produce superficial reports that provide only the most cursory review of the issuers and their finances, say industry executives and lawyers. The concept behind broker-dealers being paid a due diligence fee, usually one percent, when they sell the deal, is for "time spent to read the report and to ask questions," Kovack says. "The reality is often different," he adds, echoing other brokerage executives.

It's questionable as to whether a lot of firms even bother reading the due-diligence reports.

The bad news in the market for private placements could also signal a cultural change for some small or independent securities firms, one compliance executive notes.

"Unregistered offerings can blow up on a firm fast," says Carrie Wisniewski, president of B/D Compliance Associates Inc., which provides consulting services to broker-dealers and investment advisers. Executives and advisers with broker-dealers often think such disasters will never happen to them, she says. "In the past, brokers could talk firms into selling deals," she said. The collapse of the stock market in 2008 and 2009 changed that mind-set, at least for the moment. "Now firms are much more timid."

Local regulators with the states want changes. When Congress passed the National Securities Markets Improvement Act of 1996, it took away the power state regulators had to screen Reg D offerings and private placements. Now, the state regulators want that authority back, claiming that they have better knowledge of dubious individuals who may try to sell a bogus offering. Simply put, state regulators believe they have a bead on the local rip-off artists and know how they work. Selling private placements, state regulators believe, is a large part of the small town financial serial killer's arsenal.

"Without question, the most harmful area of state securities pre-emption has been Regulation D offerings," said Crawford in her speech. "Investors deserve better than this."

Despite such concerns, both the market and investors' appetites for such Reg D deals have ballooned.

In 2008 there were 26,485 Reg D offerings filed with the Securities and Exchange Commission, which requires scant information about the private placements. That compares with more than 11,000 such offerings in 1996. According to an SEC report, the division of corporate finance identified total estimated offerings in 2008 of $609 billion. These private deals are expensive, with investors typically plunking down $10,000, $50,000, or $100,000 just to play. They also lack liquidity, meaning once you buy, it's almost impossible to sell at an equal value, and carry risk. All the while they are lightly regulated and receive little oversight.

In 2009, more deals showed signs of stress, brokerage insiders and securities regulators say, particularly real estate deals and some involving oil and gas that could be harmed by the weak overall economy.

"We're looking at tons and tons" of offerings governed by the private placement rules, says Joseph Borg, director of the Alabama Securities Commission, who adds that the problems are numerous. "There's no gatekeeper, and the deals have gotten huge," he said, adding that small businesses are "legitimate users" for such private placement deals because these deals involve fewer regulations and less red tape. Borg scoffs at the belief that accredited investors, especially in a post-Madoff market, are supposed to know better and watch out for themselves. That thinking carries no weight with him. "It just doesn't work," he believes.

Stanford International Bank Ltd. filed its certificates of deposit offerings with the SEC under Reg D. In 2007, the bank filed a $2 billion offering with the agency. In February 2009, the SEC claimed that the bank's parent company, Stanford Financial Group, which claimed to have $8.5 billion in assets, was running a "massive Ponzi scheme" based, in large part, on publicizing and promising phony returns on its CDs. In other words, the Stanford fraud was given an aura of legitimacy using Reg D or private placement labels on top of phony investments.

• ---

Private placements are highly unregulated and brokerage firms selling them often do not investigate the soundness of the investment.

In the summer of 2009, the SEC charged two more firms with fraud related to large private-placement deals with an estimated value of $2.7 billion. On July 7, the SEC charged Provident Royalties LLC and a number of its related entities with operating a fraud and a Ponzi scheme in the sale of $485 million of preferred stock and limited-partnership offerings in oil and gas deals. The deals were sold from 2006–2009.

About a week later, the SEC charged Medical Capital Holdings Inc. with fraud in the sale of $77 million of private securities in the form of notes. The fraud appears much bigger. Brokers sold the notes to about 20,000 investors, and they were told they would receive six percent interest each year, and get their principal back in eight to ten years, as well.

Since then, a court-appointed receiver has said that $543 million worth, or about 87 percent, of all the accounts receivable Medical Capital controlled is "nonexistent." In total, Medical Capital sold $2.2 billion in notes from 2003–2008. The court-appointed receiver is trying to sell Medical Capital assets in order to pay back investors, the majority of whom will be lucky to get pennies back for each dollar invested.

Brokers and advisers have plenty of incentive to sell private placements. The broker can earn much more selling a private placement than a mutual fund. Brokers typically earn an extremely high commission of five percent to ten percent. In a mutual fund transaction, a broker can earn between one percent and four percent of the sale.

According to the private-placement memorandum for one Provident offering, the sales commission was eight percent and the due-diligence fee was one percent of the deal's total value. If Provident offered a one percent due-diligence fee to securities firms on all its deals, that means brokerage firms collected $4.9 million in due diligence fees. What constituted a securities firm's due-diligence on the Provident offerings and other deals is unknown.

In a Reg D filing for a Medical Capital offering from 2008, called Medical Provider Funding Corp. VI, for $400 million, sales commissions were slated to be $21 million, or a little more than five percent. On the filing, there is no mention of a due-diligence fee.

Due-diligence firms defend their role, saying that there is no other way for broker-dealers with limited staff and resources to sell the private offerings. They also stress that these private placements and Reg D offerings are for accredited investors, meaning investors who are both savvy and wealthy, like those who buy into hedge funds.

The private placement industry appears to harbor an Orwellian paradox in its mindset. The company selling the private placement often pays for its own due diligence. That company issuing the private placement then turns around and pays the securities firm a due-diligence fee for its brokers to sell the product, even though the securities firm may have done little or even no due diligence at all.

"The issuer pays our fees," says Bryan Mick, president of Mick & Associates PC LLO. He stressed that the due-diligence firms have a "code of professional responsibility" to maintain, and that "we represent our broker-dealer clients."

The issuers of the private placements, known as "sponsors" in the industry, can have contentious relationships with the analysts who write the due-diligence reports. After Medical Capital

Holdings blew up in July 2009, one due-diligence professional wrote in an e-mail to securities firm clients that Medical Capital was less than forthcoming with information.

"After my visit to Medical Capital [in 2008], they indicated they would require a restrictive confidentiality agreement before I would be allowed further access," Paula Miterko wrote to her securities firm clients soon after the SEC charged Medical Capital with fraud. "After months of negotiations, they still have refused to sign the agreement they requested. We have been unable to conduct further meaningful due diligence and it is unlikely we will be able to at this time."

In a later interview, Miterko stressed that her contract in this case was with a securities firm, and she was not paid by Medical Capital. The company "wasn't very cooperative," she says. It objected to the fact that she was going to show her report to more than one securities firm. After a day and a half of her questions, she said, Medical Capital executives showed her the door. "Nine times out of ten," the contract to review a deal is with a broker-dealer, not the issuer, she said.

There's no way to tally the potential cost to broker-dealers who sold clients the Provident and Medical Capital deals. Investors have begun to sue the securities firms who sold the private placements. To do so, they filed arbitration claims against the securities firms in an industry forum controlled by FINRA, the Financial Industry Regulatory Authority.

The Medical Capital saga is particularly revealing of a number of shortcomings in the marketplace when it comes to private placements. In short, they carry tremendous risk for investors, and zealous brokerage firms and advisers sometimes sell these products to investors who are unaware of what they are buying.

A look under the hood at Medical Capital shows that investors may have no way of knowing what the managers in charge of the private placement fund are doing. Medical Capital, which sold its private-placement offerings through a number of regional and small securities firms, spent freely and lavishly on assets that had nothing to do with medical receivables—its core business—according to court papers.

Medical Capital investments included $20 million for *The Perfect Game,* a film about a group of Mexican youths who in 1957 became the first foreign team to win the Little League World Series. The film stars Richard "Cheech" Marin, of Cheech & Chong and *Nash Bridges* fame.

Medical Capital also spent $7 million on a company that marketed a mobile-phone application that consisted of a live video feed of a hamster in a cage and an unspecified amount for a 118-foot yacht named *The Home Stretch.*

Remember, Medical Capital packaged medical receivables and sold them as private placements. In total, Medical Capital raised $2.2 billion from 20,000 investors to buy hospital receivables and other investments. Medical Capital bought receivables from hospitals and health care providers at a discount. Investors were supposed to profit when the bills are paid.

Like any Ponzi-type scheme, the investors who bought the Medical Capital products did see a return on some of their investment at first. Perhaps the executives at Medical Capital had a legitimate business plan and bought real businesses and receivables that generated real returns for investors. Who knows where it all went wrong, but it appears that Medical Capital began to cook its books.

According to the report from the court receiver, Medical Capital conducted numerous transactions with itself, transferring accounts receivable from one investment entity to another at least 301 times. The report identified $829 million in such transfers.

That creates "a number of potential issues," the report stated. First, some of the receivables were already old when purchased by the new investment entity, and receivables lose value as they age because the likelihood of companies and individuals actually paying bills decreases over time. Second, some of the receivables that the new investment offerings bought didn't exist. Finally, Medical Capital overstated the value of some of the receivables, according to the report.

When the SEC sued Medical Capital and Chief Executive Sidney M. Field and president and Chief Operating Officer Joseph "Joey" Lampariello, it alleged that they had defrauded investors. The SEC claimed that the two men had improperly diverted $18.5 million of investors' money and failed to tell them about several Medical Capital defaults. "It appears that note holders will almost certainly suffer significant losses on their investments," the report states.

In a response to the receiver's report, Field and Lampariello said that the receiver "did not hesitate to attack the defendants and their assets with his inchoate, tentative, and unsubstantiated analysis.

"The note holders and the court would have been better served if the receiver would have spent more time figuring out how to maximize the value of assets and less time trying to conduct discovery for the SEC and trying to provide the court with his analysis of the relative merits of the SEC's case," the response stated.

The two Medical Capital executives further said that the assertion that old receivables were sold from one investment to another was "perhaps the most ignorant statement in the entire report," adding, "this assertion is patently false."

Likewise, the motion picture asset, the boat, and the hamster video were "mischaracterized."

Medical Capital didn't have its own sales force. Selling to 20,000 investors would be far beyond the reach of such a firm.

Like other private placement sponsors, it relied on a number of small and regional brokerage firms to sell the shares. These firms in the securities business are commonly called "independent" brokerage firms. They earn that tag because advisers and brokers are not employees of large institutions, like brokers sitting in a branch office of Merrill Lynch or Morgan Stanley. Instead, these brokers are independent contractors, file tax returns as such, and are small business owners who typically have a one- or two-person office that is far away from the supervision of headquarters.

The relationship between the brokerage firms that sell the private placements and the sponsors of the products is sometimes fraught with problems, as noted earlier. Medical Capital appears to have shown that.

A former top executive at one such brokerage firm, Securities America Inc., actually feared "a panicked run on the bank" in the summer of 2008 from clients who invested in private securities of Medical Capital. Alarm bells started ringing during the summer at Securities America over the fiscal health of Medical Capital private placements. That was almost a year before the SEC charged Medical Capital and its top executives with fraud.

At that time, one client in particular of the independent broker-dealer was having difficulty redeeming shares of Medical Capital. According to a July 2008 e-mail written from a Securities America executive to a Medical Capital official, "This is beyond alarming for us," wrote W. Thomas Cross. At the time he was senior vice president of the products distribution group for Securities America. "Please see if you can find out what is going on and what we can do on behalf of our clients. I honestly fear a panicked run on the bank from Cedar Brook [Financial Partners LLC] if what they seem to be saying is true," he wrote. Cedar Brook of Cleveland is a firm affiliated with Securities America, meaning that the brokers there have their securities licenses registered with that firm.

In fact, 400 Securities America brokers sold the Medical Capital private placements, and those brokers were the largest single sales force of the product. While dozens of brokerage firms' advisers sold the notes, Securities America's advisers sold $700 million of the notes and the firm was by far the largest single distributor of the product.

Securities regulators in early 2010 started legal action against the firm for its involvement with Medical Capital. In January, the Massachusetts Securities Division filed a complaint against Securities America Inc., alleging that the broker-dealer, a subsidiary of Ameriprise Financial Inc., misled investors when it sold them private-placement securities.

According to the complaint, the broker-dealer made "material omissions and misleading statements" when it sold $700 million in promissory notes issued by Medical Capital Holdings Inc. as private-placement securities. That means, simply, the firm did not tell its clients all it knew about the private placements.

The lawsuit further alleges that as a placement agent, Securities America ignored recommendations by due-diligence analysts to share financial information, including Medical Capital's lack of audited financials, with investors.

Securities America's own executives raised doubts about the deals, but those were ignored, according to the Massachusetts lawsuit. Back in 2005, Securities America president and chief operating officer Jim Nagengast wrote in an e-mail to Cross, chairman of the company's due-diligence committee and head of sales, that he had concerns about this lack of audited financials. "At this point, there is no excuse for [Medical Capital] not having audited financials . . . it is a cost they simply have to bear to offer product through our channel," the e-mail stated, according to the complaint.

Nagengast wrote: "We simply have to tell [Medical Capital] that if they don't have financials by XXXX date we will stop distributing the product on that date. Then they can decide if its [sic] worth spending $50,000 to have [the audit] done. If they won't spend the money, that should give us concern."

Cross testified before Massachusetts regulators that the reason Medical Capital never obtained audited financials was the cost of such a review. He said this despite the fact that Medical Capital earned more than $323 million in fees from its issuance of the various private placements.

From 2005–2007, Securities America's due-diligence team discovered a number of red flags about Medical Capital, including the firm's investments of up to $50 million in equity securities of all types, and mortgage loans to companies within the health care industry but "outside MCH core expertise." The Massachusetts complaint also alleges that Medical Capital failed properly to disclose mortgage financing, conflicts of interest as a dual lender, and commercial real estate risks.

Securities America denied the allegations.

"Fifty or more other broker-dealers independently conducted due diligence, but none detected the alleged fraud committed by Medical Capital, and [all] approved and sold the Medical Capital notes," Securities America noted. "Each private-placement transaction of this type is reviewed on an individual basis to determine accredited investor status and requires evidence of eligibility to purchase the product," the firm said in its official statement.

Cross had a different version of the story. In his testimony to regulators, he said that giving advisers and their clients information about the product was simply not good for business.

"If the analyst makes a statement [about the private placements] and we put that statement in the hand of the adviser, guess what happens? Somehow that document in its infinite wisdom will find its way into the hands of an investor. . . . So somehow do you figure out a way to get it in a secured server so that nobody can see it, you know, other than advisers? The problem, even if you do that, is when you create that, guess what they can do? Hit the print screen. Then they can take that document to the investor, and that's just a bad thing."

Over a period of five years, Securities America "ignored the seriousness and severity of several material risks and issues raised by the due diligence analyst conducting a review of the Medical Capital notes," the Massachusetts lawsuit alleges. Securities America claimed that the private placements were "fully secured" and that investors should include them in their "fixed income arsenal." The firm "chose to sell more than half a billion dollars of unregistered, speculative, and high risk securities, which were draped in a mantle of safety, without disclosing all pertinent information and without highlighting all material risks regarding the securities to unsophisticated investors who purchased them. Today these same investors are left with almost worthless securities."

Meanwhile, Securities America says the securities regulators are the ones who got it all wrong. In a stinging reply to accusations that it misled investors who bought high-risk private placements, the firm in February 2010 told Massachusetts regulators that the state's lawsuit against the firm "misstates facts and miscomprehends the regulatory structure of" such deals.

The formal response claims that the Massachusetts Securities Division lawsuit against Securities America is full of holes—and that the state's regulators don't understand the workings of private placements and Reg D deals. The lawsuit "mischaracterizes or simply ignores the role of selling securities broker-dealers who are not underwriters [such as Securities America], outside analysts' reports, private-placement memoranda, subscription agreements and selling agreements," Securities America said in its formal reply to the complaint. "Having thus set up its own inaccurate version of how Regulation D offerings operate, [the Massachusetts enforcement regulators report] then misstates or omits numerous relevant facts pertaining to [Securities America's] sales of the Medical Capital offerings, portraying [the firm's] normal, legitimate conduct as actionable. The complaint should be dismissed."

Some securities firms specialize in selling certain types of products, and the private placements are no exception. When coauthor Bruce Kelly asked a CEO of a securities firm in the Midwest why he had declined to sell the Medical Capital offerings, the white-haired executive shrugged his shoulders, saying he had visited the company's offices in Southern California. "It was medical receivables," he said. "These were guys in the collections business," and the executive left it at that. What he means is that Medical Capital employees were on par with repo men.

When it comes to elite, private deals, we have to ask: *who is minding the store and protecting investors?* Securities regulators, in a typically dithering fashion, often engage in turf wars over private placements and other areas rather than focus their work on protecting American investors.

If an executive at a major securities brokerage in the summer of 2008 pushed the panic button on Medical Capital, why did it take the SEC twelve months to figure out they needed to shut the company down?

"Our presence did not contribute to the crisis. Rather, the fact that our regulatory and enforcement roles had been eroded was a significant factor in the severity of the financial meltdown," Texas Securities Commissioner Crawford said in January 2010 in prepared testimony before Congress. (Remember her? She was the regulator who said the shoddy oversight of private placement deals was harming investors.) She testified before the Financial Crisis Inquiry Commission, an independent committee that is preparing a report to Congress by the end of 2010 that is supposed to make some sense of the recent financial catastrophe.

Like many concerned with the state of the securities business, Crawford also called for restoring provisions of the Depression-era Glass-Steagall Act of 1933. That law separated banks, brokerage firms, and insurance firms from one another with the goal of preventing another Depression-level collapse of the banking system.

"Since the repeal of Glass-Steagall through the enactment of the Gramm-Leach-Bliley Act of 1999, we have seen an excessive risk-taking culture emerge within institutions with federally insured deposits," she said.

Crawford took aim at the SEC and FINRA, the self-regulatory organization that is supposed to monitor and oversee stockbrokers. "The naivete behind the view that markets are always self-correcting now seems apparent," she said. "But clearly, reliance by the investing public on federal securities regulators, self-regulatory organizations and 'gatekeepers' in the years preceding the crisis and in its midst to detect and prevent even the most egregious of frauds and deceit was equally naive."

The comments did not sit well with officials at FINRA. "FINRA has taken many steps in the wake of recent scandals to improve its fraud detection capabilities, including the creation of the Office of Fraud Detection and Market Intelligence," said FINRA Executive Vice President Howard Schloss. "It would be nice if Crawford would stop pointing fingers at other regulators, and be equally introspective about the performance of state regulators in the wake of the Madoff, Stanford, and the dozens of other frauds that have happened in states all over the country."

Crawford claimed the SEC failed to detect abuses and failed to take appropriate action despite "red flags" where similar conduct by a broker-dealer would invite SEC disciplinary action. "Far from monitoring the securities markets and securities industry in order to detect and terminate abusive and illegal practices, the SEC was often prompted into action only after state regulators had unearthed them," she said.

Meanwhile, investors who have been allegedly defrauded are wondering if they will ever get their money back.

Lessons & Takeaways

- If you invest in high-risk hedge funds or private placements, *are you prepared to lose every cent you invested in that fund or offering*? If not, don't do it.
- Hedge funds are not transparent, and they are not regulated.
- Hundreds of hedge funds have failed, and investors have lost their money.
- Hedge fund investing is for the big boys. Put your money into a hedge fund only if you can afford to lose it.
- Hedge funds are supposed to be open to only sophisticated investors. Are you a sophisticated investor? If you aren't, then don't invest in one.
- Private placements are marketed to investors in a way that makes the investor feel like he or she has some type of exclusive opportunity to invest in a company. Nothing can be further from the truth. Private placements are being sold to just about anyone who has a pulse, whether or not he or she is really qualified to make the investment.
- State securities regulators themselves have stated publicly that there is no real regulation of private placement deals. Don't make an investment in something that is not regulated.
- Do not rely on supposed "due-diligence" reports that accompany private placements. These reports are often paid for by the same company that is asking you to put your money into the private placement. Companies offering private placement investments have an incentive to tell you that everything is rosy because they want and need your money.

CHAPTER
EIGHT

Securities Regulators and Their Shortcomings: Are the Regulators Protecting You?

Bernie Madoff's $50 billion fraud and Allen Stanford's alleged theft of $7.2 billion from investors happened right under the regulators' noses.

Securities regulators' shocking lack of competence when dealing with financial serial killers such as Madoff forces comparisons to the various intelligence organizations in Washington that failed to put the pieces of intelligence together before the 9/11 attacks and the Christmas 2009 attempted airplane bombing above Detroit. Simply put, the SEC—the American investing public's SEC—missed the largest financial scam in history, even though the evidence against Madoff was handed to them. Like the CIA and FBI with terror attacks, SEC officials, and other regulators in Washington, failed to do their jobs and protect the public.

A quick reminder: the Securities and Exchange Commission is the government agency that was established after the stock market crash of 1929 to protect investors from financial scams. The agency is charged with examining and regulating financial companies to protect investors.

The SEC missed the largest Ponzi scheme in world history—the $50 billion Madoff investment fraud. Despite the fact that the SEC had examined Madoff's company numerous times and had received multiple warnings from various sources that Madoff was a fraud, the SEC didn't discover the scam. Madoff's fraud only came to light when he disclosed to his sons the truth behind his entire operation.

The SEC made five inquiries into Madoff's hedge fund in a sixteen-year period. Yet each time the SEC failed to discover the fraud. Madoff himself has said that he was "astonished" that the SEC did not discover his con and never even verified whether he was making the billions of dollars of trades that he claimed he was making—that he would *have had to make* in order to truly be carrying on his stock trading business.

The SEC has an internal watchdog, the Inspector General, who investigated the SEC's serious lapse in regulation of Madoff and then published a report of its findings. The report is scathing and should serve as a warning to all investors of how incompetent the SEC had become. *Don't think for a moment that this government regulator is effective at protecting you from frauds*, is the clear message from the Inspector General's report.

The Inspector General reported that the SEC received "more than ample information in the form of detailed and substantive complaints over the years to warrant a thorough and comprehensive examination and/or investigation" of Madoff for operating a Ponzi scheme, but completely failed to do so. The first complaint was received by the agency as far back as 1992, when the SEC was made aware that Madoff was claiming to achieve consistent monetary returns on money given to him over numerous years, without a single loss (which is virtually impossible to accomplish).

The SEC was given many other written warnings about Madoff in 2000, 2001, 2004, and 2005. The complaint that the SEC received in 2005 was titled "The World's Largest Hedge Fund is a Fraud." Certainly, the complaint could not be any louder and clearer. (It reminds us of a report handed to former President George W. Bush in August 2001. It was titled "Bin Laden Determined to Strike in U.S.")

The 2005 warning went on to detail thirty red flags indicating that Madoff was running a Ponzi scheme, a scenario that the writer said was "highly likely." The red flags included the question as to whether the investment returns that Madoff was claiming were impossible to achieve, and whether they were impossible to achieve over a consistent period of years.

In other words, a normal investment adviser like Madoff would be expected to have up and down years, but not consistently up years with virtually the same percentage return each year.

Another written complaint in the SEC's hands laid out issues that the writer said were "indicia of a Ponzi scheme." This was a clear road map for the SEC to follow, which it simply ignored. A series of e-mails given to the SEC in 2004 provided a step-by-step analysis of why Madoff must be misrepresenting his trading. The SEC examiners who read the e-mails said that they indicated "some suspicion as to whether Madoff was trading at all." Again, no action by the SEC. Later, after Madoff confessed, it was revealed that indeed he had not been trading any stocks at all for numerous years. The SEC never even discovered that this so-called hedge fund genius was not even trading stocks.

Yet another warning was sent to the SEC in 2005 in which the writer states "if my suspicions are true, then they [Madoff] are running a highly sophisticated scheme on a massive scale. And they have been doing it for a long time." Another complaint the next year advised the SEC to investigate Madoff's business because it is "a scandal of major proportion."

Many of the complaints noted that no one was able to duplicate the trading strategy that Madoff claimed he was using. Madoff's alleged ability to perfectly time the ups and downs of the stock market, which numerous people told the SEC was just impossible to achieve, was a bright red flag.

At least one of the people who rang the alarm about Madoff's fraud personally visited with SEC investigators, sat across the table from them, and spelled out the fraud in simple language complete with pictures. It could not have been any easier to understand, yet some of the SEC staff could not grasp the clear information that was presented.

The business press also sounded an alarm about Madoff. Way back in 2001, an article written in *Barron's*, a well-regarded financial publication that is available on newsstands every week, discussed how Madoff was running one of the three largest hedge funds and had "produced compound average annual returns of fifteen percent for more than a decade" with the largest fund "never [having] a down year." The article questioned whether Madoff's trading strategy could have truly achieved such consistent returns. Again, a red flag was raised. Again, it was ignored.

The SEC conducted five reviews of Madoff's operations, beginning in 1992, but couldn't smell the stench that was swirling around his office. Why not? The SEC's own Inspector General reported that the SEC investigators conducting the examinations of Madoff were inexperienced. They didn't understand Madoff's operations and didn't take the time to learn about them. They missed scores of warning signs indicating that a fraud was in high gear.

During the investigation into its blunders, the SEC confessed that it "didn't have many experienced people at all" at the time since "we were expanding rapidly and had a lot of inexperienced people" conducting examinations of firms like Madoff's. One SEC employee told the Inspector General that "there was no training," that "this was a trial by fire kind of job," and there were a lot of examiners who "weren't familiar with securities laws."

The SEC investigators were aware that Madoff's investment returns were highly questionable. The Inspector General reported that the SEC had "missed [the] opportunity to uncover Madoff's Ponzi scheme sixteen years before Madoff confessed." The SEC missed the telltale sign of fraud: "incredibly consistent returns over a significant period of time without any losses." When confronted with all the warning signs of fraud, the SEC "failed to analyze how Madoff could have achieved his extraordinarily consistent returns, which had no correlation to the overall markets."

Again, this should be a caution sign to all investors, because it is impossible to achieve the types of results that Madoff boasted, but our SEC didn't protect the Madoff investors. The SEC also missed the Stanford fraud even though it had plenty of evidence in its own offices. A report by the SEC's Inspector General said that the SEC likely knew that Stanford was running his fraud for at least twelve years, but took no action, which cost investors billions of dollars in losses. SEC examiners had concluded at least four times that Stanford's businesses were fraudulent, but each time decided not to proceed further. As early as 1997, two years after Stanford registered with the SEC, an agency examiner told the branch chief about Stanford and that he needed to "keep your eye on these people because this looks like a Ponzi scheme to me and some day it's going to blow up." That finding was followed by similar conclusions in 1998, 2002, and 2004.

The Inspector General singled out the former head of enforcement in the SEC's Texas office, Spencer Barasch, as the senior person who stamped out efforts by junior staff members to investigate Stanford. The Inspector General has recommended Barasch for possible disbarment from the practice of law.

While you are reading this, another fraud is being committed. Is our SEC finding it?

The securities regulators missed two of the largest frauds in history—Madoff and Stanford.

Financial serial killers are like cockroaches. It's extremely difficult to stamp them out. The financial services industry has many corners in which to hide, and securities regulators have done very little to aggressively track or investigate these hiding places.

There are the giant fraudsters like Madoff. We've just seen how he avoided the prying eyes of securities regulators. The smaller financial serial killers also escape the detection of securities regulators and wind up doing plenty of damage, too.

Meet Irving Stitsky. His story further proves that if investors think the securities regulators are protecting them from financial serial killers, they should think twice.

A former executive at Stratton Oakmont, (remember the Long Island "boiler room" with the parking lot that resembled an auto show?) Stitsky was found guilty of securities fraud in December 2009. That, however, happened to be more than eleven years after he was kicked out of the securities industry by a group of regulators.

Stitsky, a former managing director and junior partner at Stratton Oakmont, and two colleagues stole more than $18 million from 150 investors using phony or ginned-up private placements.

As we said earlier, in the brokerage industry Stratton Oakmont's name is almost synonymous with the phrase "boiler room." Stratton brokers in the 1990s used high-pressure tactics to sell investors an array of initial public offerings, many of which turned out to be worthless. Regulators shut the firm down and the firm's two founders pleaded guilty to securities fraud and money laundering.

Stitsky apparently couldn't stay away from the easy money. He, along with Mark Alan Shapiro and William B. Foster, later operated a group of companies under the name Cobalt, which claimed to acquire and develop real estate properties throughout the United States.

According to the U.S. Attorney's office, the three Cobalt executives lied about the company's history and caused others to lie to investors about Cobalt's ownership of certain properties. Stitsky and Shapiro also failed to tell investors they were convicted felons.

These are the kinds of guys who should be on the radar of securities regulators.

Shapiro previously served thirty months in prison after pleading guilty to bank fraud and conspiracy to commit tax fraud, according to the Justice Department complaint.

Stitsky also pleaded guilty to fraud charges, including conspiracy to commit securities fraud, wire fraud, and commercial bribery in the Southern District of New York in Manhattan and of making false statements and of conspiracy to commit securities fraud in the Eastern District of New York in Brooklyn, according to the complaint.

If investors with Cobalt wanted to check Stitsky out with FINRA they couldn't. The same regulators that barred him from the industry protected him by keeping that information private on its Web site and in its database. Because of old FINRA rules, investors could not check Stitsky's record and background in the securities business. After two years—regardless of their standing in the industry—brokers' records were taken down from BrokerCheck, a service on FINRA's public Web site. That meant a financial serial killer like Stitsky could operate knowing a prospective client could not turn to the securities industry to get basic information about him.

FINRA is a private corporation set up by the securities industry to perform market regulation. FINRA is a self-regulatory organization, meaning that the securities industry uses FINRA to regulate itself. It is not an independent government agency and is not part of the U.S. government.

FINRA regulates its members by enacting and enforcing rules that are supposed to govern the business conduct of its members. FINRA also sets up and runs the binding arbitration process that investors are required to agree to when they open up a brokerage account and sign a brokerage contract. So if you have a dispute with a brokerage firm or a broker, you can't go into the U.S. court system and have a judge or jury decide your case; you are forced to bring your complaint into an arbitration forum that is organized and run by the securities industry itself.

As we said earlier, the lack of information about financial serial killers like Stitsky has finally changed. At the end of 2009, FINRA said it had won approval from the Securities and Exchange Commission to expand the BrokerCheck service and make disciplinary records available permanently.

That's a little too late for the investors who lost $18 million to Stitsky and the agents at Cobalt.

After a three-week trial, Stitsky, Shapiro, and Foster, were found guilty of wire fraud, mail fraud, and conspiracy charges.

Although they've seemingly been sleeping on the job, securities regulators are some of the best-paid bureaucrats in Washington.

Thirteen current and former executives of FINRA made more than $1 million apiece in 2008, a year in which the regulatory organization lost $696.3 million, according to tax forms FINRA filed in November 2009, as well as the company's annual report.

The compensation, which includes salary, bonuses, and retirement plan awards, pales next to the payouts that some Wall Street executives and bankers made in boom years—but still raised eyebrows given FINRA's investor protection charter and its hundreds of millions in losses.

Despite the billions of losses to investors due to financial serial killer fraud by the Madoffs and Stitskys of the market, these well-paid securities regulators have stepped into some outstanding new jobs. The highest-paid executive was Michael D. Jones, the group's former chief administrative officer, who left in the summer of 2008 after more than a decade at FINRA with compensation, severance, and accumulated benefits valued at $4.43 million. Jones subsequently joined the Public Broadcasting Service as its chief operating officer.

Several of FINRA's 2008 millionaires have gone on to lower-paying, but extremely powerful, government positions. SEC Chairman Mary Schapiro, who received $3.3 million in 2008 as FINRA's chief executive officer, is paid $162,900 to run the government agency. In 2009, she received another $7.2 million from FINRA as part of her accumulated retirement-plan benefits.

Elisse Walter, who was appointed a commissioner of the SEC in July 2008, received $3.8 million from FINRA the same year (including $2.4 million of supplemental retirement benefits) for running its regulatory policy and programs. Internal Revenue Service Commissioner Douglas Shulman pocketed $2.7 million in salary, bonus, and retirement benefits for his eight years of service at FINRA, which ended when he joined the IRS in March 2008.

Four current FINRA executives—including enforcement chief Susan Merrill and Grace Vogel, executive vice president for member regulation—made more than $1 million in 2008, and four others made more than $800,000.

Schapiro's compensation included $20,000 for club memberships in New York and Washington, $20,000 for personal financial and tax counseling, and a car and driver for use in both cities, according to the tax form. FINRA also generally pays a "gross-up" adjustment to cover its executives' costs.

Who knows how much higher their salaries will be if they move from the public arena of securities regulation to work for Wall Street's investment banks? It's an inevitable career path for many regulators, regardless of their success or failure rate in preventing or catching financial serial killers.

The SEC is not the only group of securities regulators that bungled a huge fraud investigation of a financial serial killer.

A report from 2009 detailing FINRA's inability to detect Allen Stanford's long-running, alleged $7.2 billion fraud clearly shows that the securities industry's self-regulator has gaping and significant problems related to its examinations of securities firms.

Despite its roster of millionaires, FINRA as an institution couldn't see the Stanford fraud with any clarity until it was way too late.

In an attempt to make sense of its bungling, FINRA's board of governors appointed a committee to examine the organization's processes for the detection of fraud and Ponzi schemes. Of course, the report discusses Madoff, but the details of how FINRA bungled any potential investigation into Stanford's brokerage operations reveals an overly bureaucratic organization with employees who don't understand their roles, power, or authority.

"FINRA has to make sure that the staff is not making ultimate determinations in regard to jurisdiction, such as whether Stanford's [certificates of deposit] were securities," says Brian L. Rubin, a partner in Sutherland Asbill & Brennan LLP. "That question needs to be taken to higher levels."

Securities lawyers love to argue such points. As the Stanford case repeatedly shows, such debates can bog down an investigation and in the end harm, not protect, investors.

Again, we are about to enter the Orwellian world of the securities business. In this instance, FINRA's failure to stop Stanford means they should have had more power at their disposal, a spokeswoman says. FINRA sees the Stanford and Madoff cases as an opportunity to expand its oversight to include registered investment advisers. (More on that confusing legal and business difference in the next chapter.) "FINRA's examination program is fundamentally hampered by its lack of jurisdiction over investment advisory activities," says Nancy Condon, a FINRA spokeswoman.

According to the report, a Dallas office of FINRA had five opportunities in the forms of tips or exams from 2003–2005 that officials could have used to put a halt to Stanford's alleged scheme.

Stanford International Bank of Antigua created the certificates of deposit and sold them through its Stanford Financial Group broker-dealer in Houston.

Although the report concluded that regulators mishandled "striking" tips from whistle-blowers looking to take down Stanford, what is perhaps more worrisome is that examiners and officials appeared to lack an understanding of the basic scope of their jobs. For example, in 2005, during a routine exam of Stanford Financial Group, the lead examiner focused on the CD program and concluded that Stanford's firm was "smarter than Goldman Sachs" if it was really creating such high rates of return, the report stated.

The rest of the exam team, however, failed to nail down key facts about the firm's clients that would have given them the authority to take action against the firm without any argument about FINRA's jurisdiction. Those three junior examiners on the team each had less than a year on the job.

"A showing that the firm's customers were liquidating securities in order to buy into the CD program would have provided FINRA's staff with jurisdiction to proceed against the firm under the anti-fraud provisions of the federal securities laws," according to the report.

In other words, the examiners missed some of the most routine aspects of an exam into a broker-dealer or representative: asking how a client paid for an investment, whether it was suitable, and following that trail of money.

In the end, the lead examiner "was uncertain as to whether FINRA could show that [the CDs] were securities. The issue wasn't pursued further in the 2005 cycle exam," according to the report.

The lapses continued. Staffers, meanwhile, could have questioned Stanford personally about the CDs but didn't. He was the broker-dealer's sole director, and therefore FINRA had jurisdiction over him.

Another observer's assessment is more blunt. Bill Singer, a former FINRA attorney, says that lawyers bouncing between FINRA and well-paying jobs at large national securities firms are part of the problem, and he points to the Stanford case as particularly revealing of such "cronyism."

Did cronyism exist at Stanford?

Bernard Young was the head of FINRA's Dallas office from 1999–2003. He then went on to become the managing director of compliance for the Stanford Financial Group.

The report insists that Young's role as head of compliance at Stanford Financial had no effect on FINRA staff members.

It stated that "the interviews of current FINRA employees and review of exam files identified no information to suggest that Young's presence at the firm compromised FINRA's subsequent examination of the firm discussed in this report."

In the eyes of FINRA officials, cronyism was not a factor in the failure to nail Stanford. We disagree.

Lessons & Takeaways

- Many parts of the investment business are overseen by the industry itself. When an industry regulates itself, it is apt to gloss over problems and to hide them from the public.
- Although they are trying to take more aggressive and proactive steps against fraud, securities regulators have a history of being slow to become involved in cases. As Madoff and Stanford showed, regulators appear out of their league when confronting industry big shots.
- The regulators try to protect investors, but they are not always successful.
- It is better to invest in a regulated financial product than a nonregulated financial product.
- Regulators are human, and they can make mistakes. They missed the largest Ponzi scheme in world history—that run by Bernie Madoff.
- Financial serial killers are often clever and know how to work around the regulatory system. Do some of your own investigation, ask the hard questions, and steer away from any investment idea that sounds suspicious.

INTERLUDE

The Investment Industry Speaks

In this interlude, veteran industry executives who specialize in compliance and oversight tell readers the tricks of the trade and what to watch out for in common transactions with a stockbroker or investment adviser.

Compliance officers can be the most important—and most disliked—executives at securities firms. Their job is to remind brokers at securities firms what they can and can't do, and they often interfere with brokers racking up big commissions for sales on products when the sale simply was not done right, was not suitable, or was inappropriate.

Put another way, compliance executives are quite often the out-of-place lawyer geeks at the carnival of sales that is the financial services and securities industry. The investment product business is based on selling products to people like you—and that's it. Forget fancy taglines or advertising campaigns that focus on the sanctity of home, self-improvement, or what a smart guy you are. Compliance executives, because so many are lawyers, all think the same way. They don't want to hear about what a great guy the broker is and how often he goes to church; they just want to know whether the broker sold the suitable or appropriate product to a ninety-four-year-old widow.

Following is advice from two pros in the business, Terry Lister and Carrie Wisniewski.

Lister, general counsel for Waddell and Reed Inc., has worked as a compliance executive for every kind of securities firm, from hard-sell bucket shops to pristine broker-dealers. He has seen professionals at the top of their game, and he has seen the dregs. When it comes to the psychology of the investor, Lister, 61, says clients must keep in mind that a stockbroker or investment adviser is merely human and therefore flawed.

"First, you have to be mindful that brokers are just people," he says. "They come in all sizes and shapes and colors. Some are ethical, capable, and competent and others are the exact opposite. Just because they have a securities license and work with what we consider a reputable firm doesn't mean they are competent and reputable."

If the broker's office is luxuriously appointed, that doesn't mean the broker or adviser is successful, smart, and making money for his clients, Lister says. In fact, those are all red flags that should put the investor on notice. "You have to treat them like any other service provider—ask questions, check backgrounds, and get references," he says. Find an independent reference—from a trusted family member or close friend. Just because the entire congregation is investing with the adviser is not an appropriate reference, Lister says. It's simply a dangerous herd mentality that can lead to disaster.

Investors may choose between two types of advisers. A broker who charges a commission, and an adviser who charges a fee.

If you invest with a broker, use someone who is also helping a trusted friend, Lister says. "Rely on word of mouth from a very close friend. That's no guarantee, but it's still better than using the guy you go to church with."

If you choose an adviser who charges a fee, use the same referral process. Also look to see if they have the CFP—Certified Financial Planner—designation, says Lister. "Generally speaking, but not always, advisers with the CFP designation have higher standards and additional education and training" than those who don't. "That's a good starting point."

· ---

"And for goodness sake, open your account statements when you get them each month or quarter and make sure they make sense. Don't wait for your broker to tell you that everything has doubled."

--- ·

Madoff's revelation that he was running the largest Ponzi scheme in history floored Lister. "He was highly respected by the industry, customers, and regulators. By all accounts, he had no reason to steal people's money. He was smart, talented, and through his trading process made the OTC (over the counter) securities market more efficient. When I read about Madoff in the paper I thought I was going to pass out, literally. I thought they were dead wrong."

Carrie Wisniewski started out as a retail broker in 1985, a twenty-three-year-old rookie. Now she's the boss, an executive who runs a brokerage firm that specializes in compliance for brokers who want to outsource the task.

Her initial inexperience was an issue for some prospective clients. "Did I really understand the concerns of a fifty-year-old client, with me just in my twenties?" asks Wisniewski, president of B/D Compliance Associates Inc. "No, I didn't. Now that I'm almost there, it's a whole different mind-set."

Experience counts, she says. "You probably want a broker or adviser who's been in the business for a while, and who's been with the same firm for a while."

Be careful if your broker appears to be well-traveled and has frequently moved from firm to firm. The securities industry knows that can be a signal of a broker with problems. "A lot of times, you see a broker's records and he's been with one firm for four months, another six months, and then moved around, sometimes quite a lot." If a broker has been in the business for a while, and has never been with a firm for more than one year, the client should be wary. "If you're a good broker with a clean record, your firm is going to do whatever it takes to make you stay. They don't want you to leave. If you're up and leaving every year or every few months, it raises questions."

The first place to look for a broker's career record is on FINRA's BrokerCheck. The BrokerCheck report will show you the broker's education and employment history, registrations, as well as some disciplinary history. You should also search on Google for the broker or adviser, and see what you can find.

"I don't think it's worth it to ask for references—they're just going to give you three people they've cobbled together who will say nice things about them. I'd ask them for a résumé. I'd like to know how long they've been in the business."

A legitimate broker or adviser does not use the hard-sell techniques, Wisniewski says. The broker "shouldn't be pushy. In fact, when I was in sales, the best way to sell somebody was not to be pushy and to simply give them information and answer their questions. If somebody says, 'You have to act now!' that smells fishy. When I was in sales, I would give people information, and I wouldn't hear back from some of them in six months. They'd talk to a whole lot of financial advisers, and come back to me and say, 'You're the only one who didn't annoy the heck out of me.'"

CHAPTER
NINE

What Is an Investment Adviser and Why Are So Many Running Ponzi Schemes?

The general public generally does not understand the subtle but important distinctions between the *different titles* of professionals who sell financial services and investment products.

The financial serial killer, however, is well aware of the differences, and often uses the American system that licenses sellers of financial services to take advantage of investors' ignorance.

As we have said, broker-dealers are licensed and regulated by FINRA, the Financial Industry Regulatory Authority. Now, FINRA has deep problems, but it does some things right, too. Despite its many recent foul-ups, at times it lives up to its mission to protect investors.

For example, FINRA routinely performs examinations of brokerage firms. Depending on the size of the firm and the kind of securities business in which they are involved, FINRA examines a securities firm every one, two, or four years. The firms dread the process. They must break out the spit and polish for the examiners, show the company's trading books and account records, and provide a host of information. Indeed, the process helps keep the brokerage firms honest and on their toes.

Many in the industry criticize those exams for being too perfunctory, because the examiners work from a checklist set by the bureaucrats back in Washington, where FINRA has its headquarters. Many industry lawyers and executives believe that the FINRA examiners should work and think more independently and that if they did, they could track down alleged frauds like the $2.2 billion Medical Capital private placements scheme we described earlier.

In recent years, FINRA has also put the squeeze on many brokerage firms that employed bad or shady brokers, passing rules that require those brokers to have extreme supervision. That drives up costs for securities firms, and thus some firms have moved away from taking on brokers with compliance problems or problems with clients. We took our shots at FINRA in the previous chapter for how it bungled the Stanford matter, but FINRA should be commended here.

Financial service firms that are registered investment advisers (RIA) and sell investment advice and products to investors, however, face a lot less scrutiny from regulators. For example, they are not examined each year (a process that would drive up their operating costs). They are regulated by the Securities and Exchange Commission or the state government, and these RIA firms are examined once every eight to ten years or so.

The SEC's ineptness over the Bernie Madoff affair should be a warning to investors regarding that agency's incompetence. If the SEC had understood how to review Madoff properly, it would have greatly curtailed the biggest fraud in U.S. history.

• --

So, *where is your money*—in an account with a broker-
dealer at a brokerage firm whose books and records
are looked at every one to four years, or with an RIA
which escapes a government exam for the better part
of a decade? If you're like most people, you probably
can't answer that question, and that's what a financial
serial killer wants.

-- •

Here's a bit of quick background about the differences between
brokers and investment advisers. Congress is debating whether
everyone who sells investment products to consumers should
be held to the same standard and act in their customers' best
interests. As we said, a stockbroker charges a commission for a
sale, and an investment adviser charges a fee for advice. Over the
years, those two differences have become blurred.

"At issue is whether brokers should be required to put their
clients' interest first—what is known as fiduciary duty," the *New
York Times* reported. "The professionals known as investment
advisers already hold to that standard. Brokers at firms like
Merrill Lynch and Morgan Stanley Smith Barney, or those who
sell variable annuities, are often held to a lesser standard, one
that requires them only to steer their clients to investments that
are considered 'suitable.' Those investments may be lucrative for
the broker at the clients' expense."

While Congress created the Securities and Exchange
Commission in 1934 and gave it the authority to oversee brokerage
firms, it eventually farmed out much of the rule-making and
oversight to the predecessors of that self-regulatory (and private)

group we discussed, the Financial Industry Regulatory Authority, or FINRA.

So, advisers charge a fee and are held to a fiduciary standard of care. Brokers charge a commission, and are held to a less rigorous standard of suitability. However, brokerage firms are reviewed more frequently than advisers. It is becoming more common in the retail securities business for the salesperson to act as both the adviser and the broker. That's why the issue can be confusing to investors, and sometimes regulators, and that's just what financial serial killers count on.

There are currently 23,000 registered investment advisers operating in the United States. They are split into two types: firms with more than $25 million in assets are registered with the SEC, and firms with less than that amount in client assets register with the state. Investment advisers have a different standard of care when they sell clients products; they must act as a fiduciary, meaning that they put the client's interest ahead of their own. (Think of it as the adviser actually buying the product on your behalf.)

Remember, when a stockbroker sells a product, it must be suitable. The brokerage industry resists the legal label of fiduciary, because that label subjects them to a higher legal standard and responsibility than they currently have. The industry is afraid that, if a broker was a fiduciary, clients would have more room to sue them and therefore liability costs would increase.

The companies that employ stockbrokers hate having their salespeople called brokers. Perhaps those firms believe there is something sleazy about the "broker" title. Perhaps "investment adviser" or "consultant" sounds classier and more benign.

Perhaps every one of those broker/adviser/consultants should have some sort of subtitle, like "Remember, there is no guarantee in the stock market and I'm the guy who is putting your life savings at risk."

The confusion and the obfuscation of titles can certainly hurt investors.

Aware of this, the SEC in 2007 commissioned the RAND Corporation, a think tank, to study the financial advice marketplace. The industry was not surprised to learn that consumers had no idea about the differences and intricate variations between brokers, advisers, consultants, and anything else you wanted to call people who sold financial products.

The RAND study said that "Financial advisor and financial consultant are titles commonly used by investment adviser employees as well as broker-dealer employees. Furthermore, the most common titles of financial service providers that those respondents employ are generic terms, such as advisor or financial advisor.

"Given the growing complexity of the financial service market, we were not surprised to find that many [investors] did not understand key distinctions between investment advisers and broker-dealers—their duties, the titles they use, the firms for which they work, or the service they offer." The study concluded that, despite the confusion, most of the people who participated were satisfied with their broker or adviser.

The RAND Corporation probably didn't speak to many investors who invested with a financial serial killer like Irving Stitsky. Such brokers and advisers routinely tell people they are advisers even though they are not registered with a state or the

SEC. Called "unregistered investment advisers," these financial serial killers commonly had some kind of license to sell financial services products in the past, only to have it yanked away. That's what happened to Stitsky, but that didn't prevent him from furthering his career as a financial serial killer.

Keeping track of financial serial killers is a tricky business, particularly when they leave (or are booted from) the confines of the securities industry, but keep peddling financial products.

Here's a story of one financial serial killer who adroitly exploited the confusion between titles and boundaries of brokers and advisers and agents described above. He did so while he was being investigated by securities regulators. Again, he didn't work on Wall Street, but in the lovely coastal California town of San Luis Obispo, where many residents feel so safe they don't lock their doors at night.

Jeffrey Forrest used titles and registrations to impress clients while he allegedly stole more than $40 million from them.

Forrest's broker-dealer employer asked him to leave in 2006 after he had made improper sales of a hedge fund that spurred lawsuits from investors. Forrest's scheme appears similar to the dozens of bogus hedge funds and Ponzi schemes that began to blow up in 2007, most notably, of course, the Madoff fraud. Unscrupulous advisers held out the phony investments as dependable and predictable, with little or no volatility.

In 2005 and 2006, Forrest, who was a top producer with Associated Securities Corp., advised sixty clients to invest $40 million in a hedge fund that collapsed the next year. Two years later, the SEC sued Forrest for failing to disclose hundreds of thousands of dollars in fees he gained from the hedge fund, which blew up in 2007. The SEC suit sought to prevent him from working in the investment advisory business.

Yet, that didn't stop Forrest. He was licensed to sell insurance in California and continued to run a registered investment advisory firm, WealthWise LLC in San Luis Obispo, managing $26 million in assets. In 2009, the SEC finally barred Forrest from working as a registered investment adviser, although he could reapply in five years.

FINRA followed the SEC's lead and also took action against Forrest. He was barred from the securities industry in December 2009. The case moved slowly, as is typical. It took three years for FINRA to bar him from the business. Who knows what he may have done in that time?

Forrest's story highlights a host of vexing issues in securities regulation that interfere with its primary goal: protecting investors.

Financial serial killers too often lose one title or registration and simply hide behind another. Many in the securities industry are fed up with that fact. "If you're kicked out of one channel, you should be bumped from all," says Richard Nummi, a director with Accounting & Compliance International of New York. "I don't think [advisers] should be allowed to shop for venues."

Insurance companies, in particular, haven't been aggressive in kicking producers with potentially problematic histories to the curb.

Despite the SEC's action against Forrest and a recent loss of an $8.8 million securities arbitration claim against him, major insurance companies such as Pacific Life Insurance Company of Newport Beach, California, continued to do business with him.

In fact, Pacific Life, which owned the broker-dealer, Associated Securities, authorized him to sell insurance a month before the SEC issued a preliminary judgment to stop him from working in the industry.

When contacted by coauthor Bruce Kelly, Pacific Life said it was reconsidering its relationship with Forrest. "I appreciate you letting us know that there is still an appointment out there for Jeffrey Forrest," said Tennyson Oyler, a Pacific Life spokesman. "We are taking steps to make sure that we revoke Mr. Forrest's appointment to sell any and all Pacific Life products," he said. They eventually ended their sales agreement and professional relationship.

Additionally, a handful of other major insurance companies gave Forrest the authority to sell life insurance, including Aviva Life and Annuity Company of Des Moines, Iowa; Genworth Life and Annuity Insurance Company of Richmond, Virginia; Lincoln National Life Insurance Company of Hartford, Connecticut; and Prudential Annuities Life Assurance Corporation of Shelton, Connecticut.

These business relationships existed well after he left Associated Securities in October 2006, when executives simply "asked [him] to move on," according to transcripts from the arbitration hearing.

Financial services companies often have a hard time answering questions about the people who sell their products. They fear potential lawsuits from both the adviser and the investors, and often issue the most bland statements, even about financial serial killers, to shield themselves from liability.

When asked about Forrest, a spokesman for the insurance company Aviva said, "While we cannot discuss issues concerning specific individuals, we are currently reviewing the circumstances around this situation."

A spokeswoman for Prudential said that the company continues to monitor and review disciplinary actions against agents who sell Prudential products.

Despite the SEC's and FINRA's years of efforts to prevent Forrest from selling investors products, in 2010 he was still in the financial services business selling insurance. According to the state of California, the Mutual Insurance Company and the United of Omaha Life Insurance Company in 2010 authorized Forrest to sell various insurance products, including health insurance and life insurance. Forrest's history is littered with disputes with clients and regulators throwing him out the door, yet he has hung on to an insurance license throughout.

Securities regulators recognize that there has been a shortfall of information for investors when it comes to ex-brokers like Forrest.

In 2009 FINRA chief executive Rick Ketchum said that the regulator needs to expand its effort to keep public the records of rogue brokers.

"Individuals previously barred by FINRA and other securities regulators have surfaced in a number of recent frauds [and are] responsible for millions lost by unsuspecting investors," said Ketchum.

Once impossible to find, Forrest's records are now on FINRA's Web site under its BrokerCheck service.

According to a recent arbitration decision in which he and Associated Securities were found liable, Forrest pitched the fund, the Apex Equity Options Fund, as a safe, secure, and liquid investment.

A three-person FINRA arbitration panel in March 2009 decided that Forrest defrauded and deceived investors in that transaction, in which he collected hundreds of thousands of dollars in fees. Associated Securities was deemed liable because it did not properly supervise him.

One noted investment adviser says clients should avoid like the plague advisers who do two things: make decisions about investing the client's money and also hold the assets in custody. That combination means the adviser could get his hands on the client's money, and that could aid some type of fraud or theft.

"Never hire any form of money manager or adviser who takes custody of assets," Ken Fisher writes in his book *How to Smell a Rat: The Five Signs of Financial Fraud*. "When you hire a money manager, you should deposit the money with a third party, a reputable, sizable, big-name custodian wholly unconnected to the money manager or decision maker."

The adviser should never have custody of the assets, Fisher says. Your assets should also never be commingled or pooled with those of other investors. You should have a separate account with your name and/or your spouse's name on it. The investor also needs to get a separate account statement from the custodian as well as the adviser or broker who is running the account. (In some cases, say, if you are investing in a hedge fund or private equity fund, your money will likely be commingled with that of other investors. It will be part of the risk that you are taking on when you buy such an esoteric investment. We covered those risks earlier.)

Fisher emphasizes that both Madoff and Stanford had access to investors' funds because they controlled the custody of those funds. They built up a network of companies that gave a veneer of authenticity but in truth did no more than facilitate the fraud.

"Madoff's advisory clients (the clients he stole billions from) deposited assets directly with Madoff Investment Securities. Madoff Securities, on its own, appeared to be a legit, long-standing firm," Fisher writes. "Founded in 1960, at its height it handled $1 trillion in trades per year, making it one of the top three market makers in both NYSE and NASDAQ securities globally. That's really pretty impressive. You wouldn't logically think someone who had gotten that far in life would devolve into crime."

"But it wasn't the brokerage operation that was the problem for people. There's nothing really there to raise alarm—until the fellow with the name on the piggy bank became an asset manager, running an LLC (limited liability company) that took custody of people's money and made investment decisions for them. Then it becomes tactically nothing for him to steal, if he chooses."

Allen Stanford had a similar arrangement, Fisher notes. His Stanford International Bank was based in Antigua, where regulation and oversight were most likely lax to nonexistent. As we mentioned, the Stanford Bank issued certificates of deposit with extremely high interest rates, a definite red flag that securities regulators did not take seriously or simply failed to understand. The CDs were sold primarily through Stanford's advisory business, Stanford Capital Management, and assets were held at the broker-dealer, Stanford Group Company. "At every turn, Stanford had access," Fisher concludes.

Fisher sums it up in four points. First, insist that your assets be deposited in a third-party, credible, large custodial account which provides 24-hour Internet access. Second, insist that your assets are held in a separate account in your name alone, or jointly with your spouse or your trust. Next, never hire a discretionary money manager who holds assets at a broker-dealer he or she owns or controls. Finally, never let your assets be commingled.

Quite simply, this means never write a check to your broker in his name. If you have an investment adviser, you will write the check to the custodian, like Charles Schwab or Fidelity. If it's a broker-dealer, it will be to the bank, like Wells Fargo or Bank of America, or a clearing firm like Pershing, where your assets will be held in custody.

Fisher makes many good points in his book, but he is a registered investment adviser, not a broker, and his advice to investors is clearly biased in favor of using an investment adviser rather than a broker. The trend in the brokerage business right now is for many professionals to be both registered brokers and registered advisers—hence all that confusion around what to call your financial adviser! There are many outstanding brokers who do business both ways, and are excellent providers of financial advice.

Lessons & Takeaways

- Make sure that your money is deposited in a custodial account with your name on it, at a major financial institution.
- Insist that your money is deposited in an account with your name on it and not commingled with other people's money.
- Never give an adviser or broker the right to hold your money at an institution that he himself owns and controls.
- Never write a check to your broker or adviser in his name.
- Don't let names and titles confuse you when you seek to work with a financial professional. Ask him how he is registered, with FINRA or the SEC. Chapter Fourteen tells you how to check out his background. If he is not registered, and you can't find a history of him or his firm with regulators online, be extremely careful about giving this person your money.

CHAPTER
TEN

Mortgage Fraud: How the Mortgage Industry and Mortgage Brokers Can Rip You Off and How Promises of Investment Riches Undermine the Safety of Your Home

The housing bubble has wrecked the economy, grinding it almost to a halt in late 2008 and early 2009 as the United States dealt with the worst economic slowdown in decades.

Yet, financial serial killers made out like bandits and profited from inflating the bubble. In fact, some lawyers and investors currently speculate that the same financial serial killers who rode the real estate wave are also gaining from the crash and are currently preying on consumers primarily through two types of schemes.

First, there are mortgage brokers and mortgage company representatives (many of whom should not be licensed to do business in the industry, as we shall see) who will sell customers loan products they don't need or cannot afford, charge extraordinary and/or illegal fees and exorbitant prepayment penalties, misappropriate loan proceeds, falsify mortgage applications and loan underwriting documents (such as income and credit bureau), arrange inflated or bogus appraisals, or just simply steal the house.

Second, there are investment advisers who will convince unsuspecting consumers to borrow the equity from their home to invest with them, with the promise of returns that will not only cover the new mortgage payment but put additional money in their pocket as well. Sometimes the money is poorly invested in speculative and extremely risky ventures and lost, or simply stolen and never invested. In either case the promised returns are not realized, and if the borrowers cannot make the payments the house is foreclosed and lost.

Mortgage fraud is rampant in the United States. At the start of 2010, the FBI was investigating more than 2,800 mortgage fraud cases, almost five times as many as the 534 inquiries in 2004. Of the 2,800 mortgage fraud cases in front of the FBI, more than half (1,842) were classified as major cases, which meant they involved more than $1 million in losses. Do the math, and that's more than $1.8 billion in alleged cons, swindles, and outright thefts involving homeowners.

"Mortgage brokers are very lowlife people," says Jacob "Jake" Zamansky, one of the country's foremost lawyers representing individual investors in securities arbitration cases. Zamansky has worked to help clean up Wall Street, and hold the mortgage industry accountable for its related transgressions. As a prime example, it was Zamansky who brought the first case against a former Merrill Lynch analyst—a case that exposed the company's conflicted and fraudulent research, and eventually resulted in the New York Attorney General's well-reported $1.4 billion global research settlement with several major Wall Street firms.

"There are no federal requirements on mortgage brokers. There are very minimal state requirements. And it is questionable whose agent they are. Are they the agent for the bank? I call for a suitability standard that a mortgage broker should be held to the same standard as a stockbroker. Is this loan suitable for a customer?"

Remember, when a stockbroker sells a client a product, stock, bond, or mutual fund, he has to demonstrate that product is suitable to the investor's income, tolerance for risk, and other criteria. "There is a form that the mortgage broker fills out in which he is supposed to counsel people on whether the mortgage is appropriate to determine whether the customer is in over his head," Zamansky says, "but many mortgage brokers do no counseling. All they do is place loans."

Zamansky certainly has strong opinions about mortgage brokers, and apparently for good reason. The housing crash has put the spotlight on the quality of the brokers who put together many loans. In 2008, the *Miami Herald* ran a series of investigative articles that showed the depth of criminality in the mortgage business. The articles showed that Florida's regulators routinely failed to detect individuals who should have never been involved with the mortgage business. In fact, Florida state regulators allowed thousands of mortgage professionals with criminal records into the industry. Those financial serial killers cost consumers millions, the *Herald* report concluded.

"When Scott Almeida walked out of a federal prison and into the mortgage business, he took a gamble," one *Herald* report begins. "He admitted on his license application that he had been convicted of cocaine trafficking."

Instead of slamming the door in Almeida's face, the regulators asked the former coke dealer for a character reference. He gave them a note from his mom, the *Herald* reported. The process became truly ridiculous. Regulators told him he needed a supervisor for his practice. "He chose a guy he met in the prison visitor room," the *Herald* wrote.

The bungling continued. Regulators looking into his past asked for a copy of the court file but never demanded the police report, which shows that he had been caught with a small arsenal of assault rifles and ammunition, in addition to the cocaine.

"Their background investigation complete, regulators circled 'approved' at the bottom of the screening checklist, collected a $215 license fee and looked the other way. Over the next three years, in a crime spree that stretched from Tampa to Miami, Almeida arranged nearly $3 million in fraudulent loans and fleeced 30 people—many of them elderly and disabled."

The regulators still managed to give Almeida additional opportunities to commit crime and harm the public, according to the *Herald*. "Twice, the Florida Office of Financial Regulation— which polices the mortgage industry—failed to act on warnings that Almeida was stealing from clients, allowing his scam to thrive until police threw him in jail."

From 2000–2007, Florida regulators allowed at least 10,529 individuals with criminal records to work in the mortgage business. More than 4,000 of those cleared background checks after committing crimes that Florida law specifically requires regulators to screen for, including fraud, bank robbery, racketeering, and extortion. The *Herald* concluded that those criminals went on to commit nearly $85 million in mortgage fraud.

In October 2007, Almeida pleaded guilty to fraud, racketeering, and theft charges in a mortgage scheme that bilked millions from homeowners in Hillsborough, Pinellas, and Polk counties through lying on mortgage applications, charging illegal fees, and stealing loan proceeds from borrowers.

Unscrupulous advisers or stockbrokers at times targeted their clients' homes. For many people, a house is truly their castle, and much of their net worth is in their home. A certain kind of financial serial killer emerged during the housing boom, then again in the credit crisis and mortgage meltdown—con artist behavior used by a financial serial killer to convince clients, often elderly or desperate, to refinance or take out a home equity loan and turn over the proceeds to him. Through a proprietary strategy for creating wealth and riches, he would easily generate enough of a return to make the new mortgage payments and create a comfortable income for the client, perhaps even doubling or tripling their investment.

Here's a quick lesson: never contemplate cashing in the value of your home so some guru can invest for you. If an adviser approaches you with such a proposal, call your local police and tell them someone in your town is up to no good.

This is not just stuff in the newspaper, Zamansky points out.

"In 2007, my firm conducted its own investigation on behalf of more than a dozen Long Island and Florida working-class retirees who collectively were bilked out of millions by Peter

J. Dawson," he says. "Dawson is a once high-flying 'financial planner' who was sentenced in 2008 to serve up to fifteen years in jail. It gives me great pleasure to have been instrumental in putting him behind bars."

"Dawson, president of BMG Advisory Services, worked out of one of Long Island's most prestigious office buildings, which gave him a patina of legitimacy," Zamansky says. "Over the course of fifteen years, he convinced dozens of unsophisticated retirees to surrender their existing variable annuity policies and mortgage their paid-off homes so that he could invest the proceeds in new annuities on their behalf."

Remember Lillian Wentz, the eighty-nine-year-old grandmother whose $24 million fortune was managed by Warren Buffett? The insurance agents who convinced her to sell her stock in Berkshire Hathaway concocted a plan that was based on proceeds from variable annuities paying for life insurance. If you have an asset that has value, if you have stock or own a home, avoid any plans that are based on selling that asset to fund another kind of investment. There are simply too many transactions involved. Call a respectable estate-planning attorney to get sound advice.

"Dawson promised that these annuities would pay a higher rate of interest than their home mortgages, thereby generating additional retirement income," Zamansky says. "He assured clients that his office would pay the monthly mortgage bills."

This is where the financial serial killer really went to work, Zamansky says.

"Unfortunately for those he ensnared, he didn't invest all the mortgage proceeds. Instead, he siphoned off millions to support his lavish lifestyle, which reportedly included several properties and a lavish antiques collection. His victims are now in danger of losing their own homes because they have little or no income to cover their monthly mortgage payments; foreclosure may be imminent. The victims are mostly retired senior citizens, including a legally blind firefighter, an electrician suffering from lupus, an ailing sanitation worker, and even a priest."

Dawson did not act alone, Zamansky says. "Although Dawson masterminded the fraudulent scheme, about a dozen other mortgage companies were participants, including well-known outfits like Countrywide Home Loans and Washington Mutual, two of the nation's biggest home lenders; PHH Corp., a NYSE-listed company that has agreed to be acquired by an affiliate of the Blackstone Group and the financing and asset management unit of General Electric; and The First National Bank of Long Island.

"No doubt these mortgage company participants will dismissively invoke Sergeant Schultz's classic 'I know nothing' defense if called on the carpet," Zamansky says. "After all, there are currently no hard and fast rules or regulations requiring mortgage lenders to determine whether the loans they make are 'suitable' for their borrowers. Granted, it's quite possible that none of the lenders knew that Dawson was absconding with the monies they advanced, but they had plenty of reasons to suspect him."

Prior to starting his own firm, Dawson worked at various brokerage firms, Zamansky notes. His brokerage record, located on FINRA's Web site, contains four customer complaints, including an allegation that he induced a customer to take out a $250,000 mortgage to invest in an annuity whose interest rate was lower than the mortgage rate. "Unsuitable investments followed," according to the complaint.

Dawson's story is a searing reminder for investors to check the background of their financial professionals before ever handing over any money. In an era when access to the Web is on par with making a phone call, an investor can make an Internet check on his adviser with little effort.

Another warning sign is how he did business, Zamansky says. "The mortgage closings for Dawson's clients were typically held at his office, or in at least one highly irregular instance, a hotel room. None of Dawson's clients were represented by an attorney. Representing the mortgage lenders at most of these closings was an attorney named Ida D'Angelo or one of her associates. Ms. D'Angelo in 2006 was indicted for mortgage fraud by the Deputy Attorney General in charge of New York's Organized Crime Task Force. The indictment's complaint against D'Angelo does not pertain to her activities involving Dawson's clients."

In most instances, the mortgage monies were given directly to Dawson and not his clients. That should have raised warning signs, Zamansky says.

Dawson's clients were elderly and probably never should have been in the position to take out another mortgage, Zamansky notes. "By any standard, none of Dawson's clients should have been *granted* mortgages. They had little or no income and there was no rational reason for them to assume mortgage debt given their late stage in life, and in several instances, their poor health.

"Sadly, it shouldn't take a court order to force the defendant lending institutions to do what is so abundantly the proverbial 'right thing,'" Zamansky says. "But morals and fairness have never been the hallmarks of the U.S. banking industry, especially when there is money at stake. The Dawson case underscores why

Congress should impose suitability rules on all the nation's home lenders."

Never let the adviser commingle your funds, Zamansky says. "And make sure you understand what you are invested in. If you can't even explain it, don't do it. None of these people in Dawson could explain what he was doing. What did he do? It was a hedge fund, he was promising returns of 10 to 15 percent. Stay away."

The clients had paid off their homes, Zamansky says. "All of them. They had their homes paid off for twenty or thirty years. He said take a mortgage out on your home, he got the money, say $300,000, and promised to pay off their bills. He took the money and never paid their bills."

Lessons & Takeaways

- Never make an investment transaction that hinges upon selling your home or taking out a mortgage on your home. This is a proven recipe for disaster.
- Never be talked into a mortgage payment you cannot afford today based on potential income later—especially investment income.
- Whenever possible, deal directly with a reputable mortgage lender rather than a broker, especially one with whom you are not familiar and for whom you cannot review and verify references.
- Many states have very minimal requirements to becoming a licensed mortgage broker; some states do not even have a licensing requirement. In addition, banks vary widely on how much due diligence they perform prior to placing a mortgage broker on their approved list. The governmental agencies and mortgage lenders are not necessarily looking out for you.
- Even though it can be painstaking, confusing, and you may not understand everything you read, review the documents put before you for signature carefully before you sign. Take as much time as you need; do not let yourself feel pressured or rushed. Be wary of a closing agent who wants to rush through, not answer your questions, dismisses your concerns, or objects to you having representation present.
- In order to protect your home, do not refinance or take out a home equity loan to refinance consumer debt (credit cards, cars, boats, unsecured term loans, etc.) unless absolutely necessary. It extends the term of the debt.

CHAPTER
ELEVEN

Affinity Fraud, or Holy Rolling, Religious Zeal, and the Art of the Steal

The person you pray with, and sometimes the loudest voice in the choir, may want to steal your money. This is an extremely sad truth, and some readers will be shocked to hear it.

Fraudsters and con artists don't only focus on upper-class WASPs at the country club—the snobs from movies like *Caddyshack* who look like they can afford to be ripped off. Financial serial killers will steal from all sorts of people, usually those they know, and know well. People from all economic, ethnic, and religious backgrounds are in peril. Ethnic groups, minorities, and working-class people are increasingly becoming targets of scams, along with the upper classes.

This is nothing new. Remember Enrique Perusquia, the Paine Webber financial serial killer who was so successful he didn't even have to show up at the office and who stole divorce settlement money back from his ex-wife? The financial serial killer who was caught because, when he stole money, his forgeries of clients' signatures were too perfect? His fraud was a classic affinity scheme; his victims hailed from the same background, the upper crust of Mexico, and many victims were friends with Perusquia's father and therefore knew the financial serial killer for most of his life. In March 2010, the SEC brought actions against two sets of alleged financial serial killers who were targeting Cuban Americans and retired bus drivers in Los Angeles, demonstrating that every kind of group is at risk.

Right now, investors must guard their money more than ever. The general public lacks trust and confidence in the stock market and the economy in general after the financial crisis and the revelation of so many investment scams. That means they may seek financial advice from friends, neighbors, or people with whom they go to church. That means investors could fall prey to these increasing cases of affinity fraud.

The U.S. government recognizes the severity of affinity fraud, particularly as it relates to the small investor and Ponzi-type schemes.

"Affinity fraud refers to investment scams that prey upon members of identifiable groups, such as religious or ethnic communities, the elderly, or professional groups," the Securities and Exchange Commission said in an alert to investors in 2009, right in the middle of the wave of Ponzi schemes collapsing. "The fraudsters who promote affinity scams frequently are—or pretend to be—members of the group."

You are not safe just because you give your savings over to a member of the group you identify with most closely, the SEC contends. "They often enlist respected community or religious leaders from within the group to spread the word about the scheme, by convincing those people that a fraudulent investment is legitimate and worthwhile. Many times, those leaders become unwitting victims of the fraudster's ruse."

The scam artist exploits the trust and friendship that is a key ingredient to binding the group together, the SEC says. "Because of the tight-knit structure of many groups, it can be difficult for regulators or law enforcement officials to detect an affinity scam. Victims often fail to notify authorities or pursue their legal remedies, and instead try to work things out within the group. This is particularly true where the fraudsters have used respected community or religious leaders to convince others to join the investment."

Following is a list of the headlines from an SEC written warning in 2009 about affinity fraud. It includes a wide variety of people. The conclusion is clear: Just because you are from a certain background, practice a certain religion, or live in a certain part of the country, is no reason to think financial serial killers don't live next door to you.

PONZI SCHEME SOLICITED ELDERLY MEMBERS OF JEHOVAH'S WITNESS CONGREGATION.

FRAUDULENT REAL ESTATE INVESTMENT SCHEME DIRECTED AT RETIREES.

PONZI SCHEME TARGETED AFRICAN-AMERICANS AND CHRISTIANS.

CALIFORNIA INVESTMENT ADVISER BILKED KOREAN INVESTORS.

ARMENIAN-AMERICAN COMMUNITY LOSES MORE THAN $19 MILLION.

CRIMINAL CHARGES AGAINST SOUTH FLORIDA MAN FOR $51.9 MILLION FRAUD (INVOLVING AFRICAN-AMERICANS).

"CHURCH FUNDING PROJECT" COSTS FAITHFUL INVESTORS OVER $3
MILLION.

BAPTIST INVESTORS LOSE OVER $3.5 MILLION.

MORE THAN 1,000 LATIN AMERICAN INVESTORS LOSE OVER $400
MILLION.

125 MEMBERS OF VARIOUS CHRISTIAN CHURCHES LOSE $7.4 MILLION.

$2.5 MILLION STOLEN FROM 100 TEXAS SENIOR CITIZENS.

The SEC issued that warning in September 2009. A month later
it was suing a group for running a Ponzi scheme and affinity
fraud that targeted Haitian-American investors. The leaders of
the alleged scheme, Ronnie Eugene Bass, Jr., Abner Alabre, and
Brian J. Taglieri, used a business called HomePals Investment
Club LLC and HomePals LLC to raise millions of dollars through
false promises.

The SEC's lawsuit alleges that from April 2008 to December
2008, the defendants raised at least $14.3 million through the sale
of unsecured notes to hundreds of Haitian-American investors
by promising guaranteed returns of 100 percent every ninety
days. (The claim of such spectacular returns is practically lifted
from the Ponzi playbook.) The defendants claimed they were
able to generate such incredible returns through Bass's supposed
successful trading of stock options and commodities. (Another
claim that the financial serial killer loves to make—using options
and commodities means that he is a really smart guy, and therefore
you have nothing to worry about.)

The SEC's complaint further alleges that, in reality, Bass traded
no more than $1.2 million of the $14.3 million raised, generated

trading losses of 19 percent, and that HomePals used the bulk of the investor funds to repay earlier investors in typical Ponzi fashion. The SEC also alleges that Bass, Alabre, and Taglieri misappropriated at least $668,000 of investor funds for personal use. At the same time, federal prosecutors announced criminal indictments charging Bass, Alabre, and Taglieri with securities fraud, conspiracy to commit securities fraud, wire fraud, and money laundering.

The HomePals Ponzi scheme and its Haitian-American victims list reads almost identically to dozens of similar schemes that surfaced in the past few years. When someone from your community or church approaches you with a "can't miss" investment opportunity, take a moment and complete the following exercise: Think.

• --

Affinity fraud targets people of similar background, be it a religious, ethnic or social group.

Affinity schemes are the central focus in these cases, whether it is Madoff stealing billions from wealthy Jewish people and charities or Haitian-Americans being preyed upon by one of their own, says Jake Zamansky.

"I think we see a pattern emerging, and it's truly ethnic based," he says. "We did deal with what was a major Indian-American scam and that is the commonality. How do we avoid this? Number one, just because somebody has the same background—ethnic, religious, social—as you, that is not a reason to give him your money or to let your guard down. People need to know that this actually is a red flag."

Zamansky repeats a technical point we made earlier: if you give someone from your affinity group money for an investment, make sure that the money is held in a custodian bank with your name on it and a separate account number. "If you are going to invest with anyone, make sure that the money is at Schwab with an account number," he says. Schwab or some other custodian or bank will send you an account statement. "If that is not the case, you are asking for trouble," Zamansky says.

Financial serial killer Peter Dawson, whom we discussed last chapter, used his affinity group to create his Ponzi scheme based on a mortgage scheme, Zamansky says. "Pretty much everyone met Dawson through church. He had been an altar boy, and he called them uncle so-and-so, aunt so-and-so. Dawson's pitch was to take out a mortgage, and this is subprime borrowing, his client's paying 5 to 6 percent. He tells them he will pay the mortgage because he's making 15 percent on the hedge fund. That is all they knew, and they trusted the guy."

The advisers at Stanford International Bank used religion, and religious zeal, to sell CDs to customers. Team leaders quoted the bible when motivating the sales team to sell CDs that the SEC has now called phony. "We all seem to be of common yolk," said Hank Mills, forty-nine, a former Stanford financial adviser. The sales people "seemed to be involved in their community, in churches." In a training video, Mills recounted how he received a phone call from a dying man who then agreed to have Stanford manage his money: "We prayed together. He shares his financial picture, and he decides I'm the person that he wants to involve with his family to take care of them when he leaves."

John Moscow graduated from Harvard Law School and went to work in the Manhattan District Attorney's office, where he prosecuted frauds for twenty-eight years. Much of his time was spent prosecuting and supervising the prosecution of people in the brokerage industry. His division at the Manhattan District Attorney's office won convictions of hundreds of brokers.

He still handles white-collar fraud cases, but now at a private law firm, where he works on everything from embezzlements to international bank frauds. Moscow has spoken to and worked with the victims of financial frauds. He has seen firsthand the effects of financial fraud on victims.

In one bank fraud case Moscow saw the effects of affinity fraud. There it involved people from the Indian and Pakistani communities. "With some of the frauds that we had in the United States, they were focused on particular ethnic groups where the swindlers would go and insinuate themselves into the lives of a subset of our general community. Whether it be Latvians in south Ohio, or whatever, they would get in to the group and they would offer them opportunities, because they shared certain values. *You too will be allowed to invest in this deal.* And the deal is terrible, and you get taken for a ride. Money gets stolen. And everybody you know who thought they knew and trusted the people they were dealing with made a mistake. Why? One swindler persuades one insufficiently careful person to vouch for him, and so forth."

"Frequently you will find that the swindler goes to someone who has been very successful in one line of endeavor, but does not know the line in which the swindler is working. And he will play up the ego, he will talk about skill, he will talk about how good and skillful he is to the mark. The mark in this case is not needed for his money, but for his references."

"Bear in mind the swindler wants to be able to expand his number of victims and keep moving, so will have someone who will come in and target an influential member of the community. They will contribute to the same charities. They will approve the same ideas. They will support this person in various ways. They will appear to be generous and honest and giving. And the purpose will be to get the support of somebody respected in the community, so that people in the community with money will trust this con man with their money."

You see this particularly in communities where leadership is centralized. "If the leader is persuaded—and I am thinking here about some of the Hasidic communities—that a con man is a good man, the leadership will cause their members to support him. Because the appeal is frequently ethnic and frequently religious. Whether it's to Masons or whomever, the thought is planted that it's us against the outside world. You foster the attitude that we have secrets. You might hear 'this is a really good deal—you can't tell anybody. This is really, really hot stuff. We have to keep it secret. You can't discuss it.'"

"With that, when it turns out the con man was a swindler, the people who were in on the secret have been compromised because they haven't told their buddies quite a true story. Perhaps they got gifts out of this. Perhaps they were entertained, whether properly or improperly. It happens, and you end up where your leadership is compromised. The hardworking people who have saved their money are victimized. The integrity of the group has to be defended, so you can't tell law enforcement—you can't put the word out. Without the word going out, the con man goes off and does it again."

Lessons & Takeaways

- Be skeptical of any investment opportunity that is not in writing, the SEC advises. Fraudsters often avoid putting things in writing, but legitimate investments are usually in writing. Avoid an investment if you are told they "don't have the time to reduce to writing" the particulars about the investment. You should also be suspicious if you are told to keep the investment opportunity confidential.
- As always, be wary of "guaranteed returns" and promises of spectacular profits.
- Do your own research online.
- Fraudsters are increasingly using the Internet to target particular groups through e-mail spams, the SEC warns. If you receive an unsolicited e-mail from someone you don't know, containing a "can't miss" investment, your best move is to pass up the "opportunity."
- Simply because you attend church or synagogue with someone does not alone make that person qualified to handle your money. Financial serial killers will even use religion to con you out of your savings.

INTERLUDE
C

The Investment
Industry Speaks

A top-ranked investment adviser tells readers what to watch out for when picking a broker, planner, or investment adviser.

Paul Comstock is the founder of Paul Comstock Partners, a fee-only registered investment adviser. Comstock's company advises buyers of financial services by assisting them in determining what financial products to buy, and the quantities to buy, monitoring the investments, assessing the risk level of particular investments, and deciding whether the investments are performing as expected. Comstock helps his clients determine what their investment structure should look like based on their cash flow needs and the time frame for their investments.

He works with extremely wealthy people, and a client account on average has $8.9 million. In total, he manages $1.1 billion in client assets. A registered investment adviser, he is registered with the Securities and Exchange Commission.

When Comstock assesses a client's needs he wants to know the purpose for which his customer is accumulating wealth. Maybe it's for a retirement home or a child's education. He looks at his customers' monthly cash flow and the money they need to live on or to meet their business needs. Almost all of his clients are living off their financial assets. They're often not employed—they aren't receiving a salary from anyone—so they have to determine how much they will be earning off their assets and whether they will generate enough income to pay all their expenses. He helps his clients to develop a budget, too, looking at whether they are spending too much of their savings and whether they need to adjust their expenses to a level where they are living within the income being generated by their portfolio.

Comstock says that most of his clients are busy with personal interests or business pursuits and don't have the time to manage their money on a daily basis. Most of his clients are wise enough to know that they don't have the expertise necessary to manage money, so they seek professional advice.

Most people pick a financial adviser based on a referral from a friend or relative. "They meet someone in a social setting or affinity group like their church or synagogue," says Comstock, "and then say 'well, I need some help,' and they think this is a good guy."

To avoid being sucked into a fraud, Comstock believes that anyone looking for a financial adviser should make decisions that are "not based on trust." "That's a very important concept, because that's where we run into problems."

That was the situation with Madoff, where people selected him as their adviser because they thought he was a good guy and that they could trust him. Had they done some serious, dispassionate research and due diligence into him, they likely would not have invested with him.

"Often we begin dealing with someone who is our next-door neighbor who we think is a good guy—we see him at a social function and everybody seems to like him—but we really don't know his background." It may not be that this person is being devious or trying to scam us, but the person who wants to handle our money may just not be skilled at doing so. They may have biases. They may have conflicts of interest in their recommendations that put us at risk.

So the first thing Comstock suggests is to not enter into a relationship or make decisions based on trust and trust alone. "You want to eliminate the need for trust in the relationship. As you do that, the odd thing about it is that you will actually develop trust over time."

Another very important point is that when you invest your money, as we have pointed out before, make sure you know where the assets are physically being held. "I would recommend very highly that the assets not be in the possession of the person managing them. For instance, if you hire a money manager, know where the assets are that the manager is working with, and make sure that they are with a third-party custodian. For instance, you could use a bank to hold the assets and have an outside party manage them. You could have a brokerage house, a national brokerage house, hold the assets, and you could have outside managers run them. That is one thing that I would suggest always be part of the process—that the assets go to bed at night someplace different from the place where the assets are being managed."

Comstock continues that not only do you need to know where your assets are "but you also need to make sure that there is an independent audit of that custodian to verify that those assets that are yours are in fact there." In most situations involving fraud, such as the Madoff situation, there was no third-party verification that those assets were in fact there.

Financial advisers may have conflicts of interest, so look out for those. "Start out with the old Latin saying, *caveat emptor* or buyer beware. Never is that more true than in buying financial service products—investment products, insurance products, what have you. Conflicts of interest abound."

We have seen a huge growth in the number of people who call themselves financial advisers or financial consultants, Comstock says. They used to be called stockbrokers or life insurance agents. Now their titles have morphed into titles that suggest that they are offering independent advice, when in fact they are not. The fact is that these people are often just salesmen for financial products that their company is developing and selling.

Comstock warns that "we have to be careful that, once we ask someone for advice on what to do, the moment we implement that advice, do we know where we are implementing it? If we pull the trigger through the person who recommends it, is there a conflict of interest? For instance, does this person work for a firm that sponsors mutual funds—a bank—a private wealth adviser at a bank who says 'I think you ought to put your money in these different investment categories,' and when you do it you are doing it with a proprietary mutual fund that the bank offers?" That could be a conflict of interest that is not in your best interest.

At this point you need to investigate and ask a number of questions. Are those recommended funds priced appropriately? Are there other investments that would be better for you? Are there investments within that institution that are not being offered because they pay the adviser a smaller commission? Is the adviser offering you a particular financial product that his company created because it pays him a higher commission than a product that is outside his company?

With regard to proprietary management products (i.e., those that the company has created and is selling) there is a potential for a conflict of interest, and it should be looked at and disclosed. Comstock explains a proprietary product as one "where I as the institution—a Morgan Stanley, a Goldman Sachs, a Merrill Lynch, a J.P. Morgan Chase—put together an investment vehicle like a mutual fund. Most of the banks now have proprietary mutual funds. They make that product in house. They develop the product, they register the product, and then they sell the product to their customers. When you buy that product, you buy it through that institution. They structure the compensation within that product and the expenses that are charged against that product. So you could buy, for instance, a Columbia fund that was for some time the fund group of Bank of America. They have since sold Columbia funds off to another firm, but if you went into Bank of America and they said 'here, we'd like to put you in these mutual funds,' and they're Columbia funds, those funds were owned by and run by Bank of America. They were a distributor of their own product to their customers."

"You should know exactly how much the adviser is being paid to sell the product, how they are being paid, whether the advice is contingent on you buying the product, and if you buy it do they get a commission? What is the amount of the commission? If you buy this product, how much will the adviser make in total? And is that reasonable for the level of service and advice you receive?"

When an investor goes to an insurance company or brokerage house for investment advice, the courts have typically said that those advisers owe a legal duty to their employer, and they only have a suitability responsibility to the client. So there are different standards of accountability, and investors need to understand that. As we have stressed, we are not suggesting that insurance advisers or brokers are bad people, but we are saying that they may give advice that is foremost in their best interest; your interests may come second.

According to Comstock, some of the most egregious conflicts of interest seen today are those involving trusts. "If you are the beneficiary of a trust, and your trust is held at a commercial trust company—a bank typically—we are seeing cases where the trust company is giving advice on running the trust, while at the same time investing the trust's funds in the company's own proprietary products. We think that there is a fairly significant conflict there, because the trust company is a fiduciary, but they might be putting their interests first by selling their own proprietary products. My advice is that you have legal counsel who is familiar with fiduciary law assist you in being certain that the advice you're given from your trustee—how they're running the trust—does not involve a conflict of interest."

"We've also seen situations, for instance, where a bank trust company is running a trust with a significant amount of money in it. The customer, who is the beneficiary of the trust, will want to purchase a home. The bank trust company will advise him to take out a mortgage with the bank, when the better course of action would have been to take cash from the trust to purchase the home." What bothers Comstock here is that the bank may not advise using cash from the trust for the home purchase because the bank will have less money on hand to manage, and will not earn fees for itself from the mortgage. Again, conflicts of interest drive the bank to recommend a course of action to its customer that benefit the bank's financial interest first, and not those of its customer.

Finally, Comstock reminds us that no one cares more about our own money than we do. No one will safeguard your savings as well as you will. "We need to understand that nobody is really watching out for us. The accounting firms really aren't watching out for us. The law firms that give advice to the advisory firms really aren't looking out for us. We need to look out for ourselves."

"There is a great, great piece of advice in the Old Testament, in Proverbs. It's repeated three times. It says that in a multitude of counselors there is safety. And if there is anything at all that I could advise a client to do, it is to make sure that you have multiple opinions and perspectives looking at a financial decision before you make them. Have your attorney, your accountant, the financial adviser all give you advice. Get a second opinion from another financial adviser. Just make certain that you have a multitude of opinions before you make that financial decision, and you're probably going to make a safer decision."

CHAPTER
TWELVE

Wall Street: It's a Game for Insiders—and Outsiders, Like You, Should Get Advice

This book is for investors who want to protect their life savings and avoid con men. The more you know, the better you will be able to avoid the financial serial killer. Therefore, we must take a look at the broad stock market and ask how it gives so much to the select bankers, brokers, traders, and hedge fund managers who earn their living there while it creates so much pain for average investors.

So, when someone now offers you a "guaranteed product with returns of 12 percent, year after year, until doomsday and even after," your response will be, *that's impossible, and this is why.*

To show the little guy or gal why they have no clout on Wall Street, we first point to a short, four hundred-word or so article buried on page C5 of the *Wall Street Journal.* The date is October 22, 2009, about thirteen months after the federal government bailed out Wall Street banks with hundreds of billions of dollars of emergency aid that prevented them from collapsing. While many argue convincingly that the bailout needed to happen to prevent another Depression, it also helped titans like Goldman

Sachs CEO and Chairman Lloyd Blankfein and Morgan Stanley Chairman John Mack avoid being fitted for suits made from a barrel.

So, here's a little story, buried on a nothing page, about the annals of Wall Street and money in America. It begins like this.

The Securities and Exchange Commission proposed rules that would give the public broader information about what goes on in "dark pools," which match big stock orders privately.

The SEC's proposals, made by a 5–0 vote of commissioners, were aimed at shedding light on a corner of the market often used by institutional investors. Regulators believe private trading may put average investors at a disadvantage.

"We should never underestimate or take for granted the wide spectrum of benefits that come from transparency," said SEC Chairman Mary Schapiro. (Remember, she made millions when she was in charge of FINRA, the private regulator of the securities business, and she was in charge of that organization when Madoff stole and Stanford allegedly stole billions of dollars.)

You may owe a debt of gratitude to John Bogle and not even know it. The founder of mutual fund giant the Vanguard Group, Bogle created the first indexed mutual fund for everyday investors in 1975. It's called the Vanguard 500 Index Fund, a low-cost basket of stocks that tracks a broad index of companies. For low fees, average investors have exposure to the broad market. Bogle's little invention certainly did catch on. At the end of 2009, U.S. investors had $882 billion invested in such funds.

Putting money into such "indexed" stock funds is about as efficient a way as possible to invest in the market and keep your money out of the hands of a financial serial killer. As we shall see, stocks historically rise over a long period of time, and indexed funds capture that increase. Of course, they also capture the sharp downdrafts of the market, so they can be painful to watch, too. A financial serial killer will never tout such a fund; it's too pedestrian. There is no razzle-dazzle to entice the clients. Financial serial killers promise riches or a surefire way to beat the market. There's no such hype or heady talk around stock index funds.

In October 2008, a month after the financial crisis almost destroyed Wall Street, and one year before SEC chairman Mary Schapiro commented on getting more information about hidden stock trades, Bogle gave a speech in New York about the current nature of the stock market. He spoke to alumni of his high school, Blair Academy, and their guests. Because he's not a Washington regulator like Schapiro, Bogle does not have to worry about mincing words for fear of offending anyone. He gave a savage but profound take on the stock market, and ample reasons for most small investors to stand on the sidelines when it comes to playing this game.

Following are excerpts from Bogle's speech:

> "Since the dramatic fluctuations of the stock market, however meaningless—I have described them after Shakespeare as 'a tale told by an idiot, full of sound and fury, signifying nothing'—tend to command our attention, I propose to begin with some much-needed perspective on what investing is all about. I do so by quoting from my second book, *Common Sense on Mutual Funds: New Imperatives for the Intelligent Investor*, published almost a full decade ago.

Investing is an act of faith. We entrust our capital to corporate stewards in the faith—at least with the hope—that their efforts will generate high rates of return on our investments. When we purchase corporate America's stocks and bonds, we are professing our faith that the long-term success of the U.S. economy and the nation's financial markets will continue in the future.

When we invest in a mutual fund, we are expressing our faith that the professional managers of the fund will be vigilant stewards of the assets we entrust to them. We are also recognizing the value of diversification by spreading our investments over a large number of stocks and bonds. A diversified portfolio minimizes the risk inherent in owning any individual security by shifting that risk to the level of the stock and bond markets.

Americans' faith in investing has waxed and waned, kindled by bull markets and chilled by bear markets, but it has remained intact. It has survived the Great Depression, two world wars, the rise and fall of communism, and a barrage of unnerving changes: booms and bankruptcies, inflation and deflation, shocks in commodity prices, the revolution in information technology, and the globalization of financial markets. In recent years, our faith has been enhanced—perhaps excessively so—by the bull market in stocks that began in 1982 and has accelerated, without significant interruption, toward the century's end. As we approach the millennium, confidence in equities is at an all-time high.

Excessive confidence in smooth seas can blind us to the risk of storms. History is replete with episodes in which the enthusiasm of investors has driven equity prices to—and even beyond—the point at which they are swept into a whirlwind of speculation, leading to unexpected losses. There is little certainty in investing. As long-term investors, however, we cannot afford to let the apocalyptic possibilities frighten us away from the markets. For without risk, there is no return."

Bogle then continued with his speech:

"For example, over the past hundred years, the return on stocks has averaged nine percent per year—four percent from dividend yields and five percent from earnings growth."

"But in the very long run, speculative returns account for nothing—zero. Speculation simply reflects the optimism or pessimism—the hopes and the fears—of the mass of investors, reflected in the 'expectations market' rather than garnered through the stern arithmetic of the 'real market' of investment returns—authentic earnings growth and dividend yields."

"In this sense, as I wrote in my 2007 book *The Little Book of Common Sense Investing,* 'the stock market is a giant distraction to the business of investing.' Of course it is!"

"During the recent era—right up to this very day—an orgy of short-term speculation has overwhelmed the wisdom of long-term investing by amounts never seen before."

"Much of the responsibility for the crash in prices can be laid on Wall Street. Investment bankers, brokers, and money managers shifted their attention away from honoring, first and foremost, the interests of their clients and toward increasing their personal wealth and the earnings of their [largely publicly held] firms. Their creation and promotion of infinitely complex credit instruments (often debt obligations collateralized by mortgages, known as CDOs) led to the mass marketing of mortgages of dubious creditworthiness bundled in packages."

"But there is another, far more subtle force, that has played a huge role in the orgy of speculation that affects our fiscal markets. During the past half-century, the very nature of capitalism has undergone a pathological mutation. We have moved from an *ownership society* in which 92 percent of stocks were held by individual investors and only eight percent by financial institutions, to an *agency society* in which our institutions now hold 76 percent of stocks and individuals hold but 24 percent. It is these agents who have been the driving force in changing the central characteristic of market participation from *long-term investment*—owning businesses that earn a return on their capital, creating value by reinvesting their earnings and distributing dividends to their owners— to *short-term speculation*, essentially trading stocks and betting on their future prices. It is not only hedge funds that are playing this game, but most mutual funds and many giant pension plans."

"Wall Street marketers and entrepreneurs loved this new system, ignoring its destruction of their clients' wealth and wallowing in the wealth it generated for themselves. Revenues of our stockbrokerage firms, money managers, and the other insiders soared from an estimated $60 billion in 1990 to some $600 billion in 2007. For the outsiders—the market participants as a group, who inevitably feed at the bottom of the food chain of investing—that enormous sum represents a truly staggering hit to their earlier gains in the bull market, and a slap in their face in the bear market that followed. Any confidence in Wall Street that these participants once may have had has largely vanished, just as it should have."

"But it is up to Wall Street to lead the way to restoring the confidence of investors; even more, to move the financial sector away from the extraordinary popular delusions of crowds and the madness of speculation, returning to the wisdom of long-term investing."

"We need to return capitalism to its traditional roots as a system focused on long-term investing, not short-term speculation. For as the great British economist John Maynard Keynes reminded us more than seventy years ago, 'When investment becomes a mere bubble on a whirlpool of speculation, the job of capitalism will be ill done.'"

"Especially at this dire time, that is the one thing that our nation cannot afford."

> • --
>
> Large institutions own most stocks and they influence
> stock price movements up and down.
>
> -- •

Jim Rothenberg, sixty-five, is a Wall Street professional uniquely
qualified to comment about short-term speculation in the stock
market and how it works.

He is a walking, living history of stock trading and knows
as well as anyone how insiders can manipulate the price of a
stock. Rothenberg's father ran a stock-trading firm on the floor
of the New York Stock Exchange, Rothenberg/Stonehill, one
of many that focused on the buying and selling of a handful of
stocks. Before today's electronic trading, firms like Rothenberg/
Stonehill were the ultimate buyers and sellers of shares of major
U.S. corporations like IBM and General Motors.

Rothenberg started working in the summer for his father's
firm on the floor of the exchange in 1959 when he was fifteen.
He has had a variety of important jobs in the securities business
ever since. Most importantly, he has worked on the business
side of securities dealing and also as a securities regulator,
so he understands how foxes come to work as guards for the
henhouse.

Fifty years ago, he worked as a runner on the floor during
the summer, shuttling stock orders back and forth between
the traders. He wanted to be a lawyer, so after passing the
bar he went to the SEC in 1970 as an enforcement attorney
in the mutual fund area. Then, he chased the penny stock-
broker-dealers in New York in the 1980s. The New York Stock
Exchange, another self-regulating body like FINRA, hired him

as chief counsel of market surveillance. He then went back to his roots, returned to the floor of the exchange, and was a specialist market maker for ten years. "Fifty of my sixty-five years have been in the securities market," he says proudly. "I mean there are people who have been in the market fifty years, but they're too old and tired."

Trading stock is in the Rothenberg blood. "Dad worked for other firms when he first started, but essentially went out on his own, and I joined his firm. I spent ten years on the floor as a specialist trader. I think I'm the only one in the country—an attorney—who has done that. That's an unusual combination. And the only reason it happened was because my father was a specialist." The nepotism found so often in the securities business paid off for Rothenberg. "Otherwise there would have been no possibility of [working as a specialist]," he says.

The business used to be family-oriented, he says.

"Family and the clerks. Family would come in with specialist clerks who were good traders even though they weren't supposed to be traders. They had a good aptitude for the market and were promoted to become junior specialists in the firm. The head clerk who ran the most active stocks—had the best feel for stocks— would work very closely with the specialist trader, and they could determine who had the aptitude for it and who didn't."

Rothenberg knows the number of ways the price of a stock can be manipulated. Right now, Rothenberg believes that the impact of technology on stock trading is making the discovery of cheating harder to detect. Securities regulators are not up to speed with the latest trading technologies that hedge funds and other highly sophisticated investors use to cover their tracks and make a stock move the way they want it to, up or down.

First, Rothenberg looks back at classic signs of stock manipulation.

"Stock manipulation is much easier to accomplish in small companies that are illiquid, meaning there's not a lot of buying or selling," he says. "With large companies it's very tough to manipulate the stock price, say of an IBM or Exxon."

Individual investors should avoid such small, illiquid companies, because the biggest money managers want no part of them. "Huge institutional buyers like money managers for pension funds are buying tremendous quantities of big, large cap stocks like IBM or Exxon. You can move the price of a large stock, but you can only move it slightly, by fractions at the end of the day."

A small company that could have its stock price manipulated likely has one or two or three million shares, maybe five or ten million shares at the most. Watch out for such "thinly traded" stocks, he warns. Financial serial killers sometimes use them to take advantage of investors.

"They trade less than 10,000 shares a day, where the float, or the shares that are held by the public, and are available for trading, is tied up with a couple of large holders. And any action of stock can either crush the stock or move it. Watch out for very small companies, ones where you can buy a lot of stock at 10 cents, 15 cents, or 20 cents a share and run it to $2 or $3 and sell it."

One basic technique to manipulating the price of a stock is through rumor, he says. "The Securities and Exchange Commission has brought a number of enforcement cases, and a number of criminal proceedings by the Justice Department, that were based on rumors. The answer is that sometimes it is a group of brokers within one firm or a group of brokers that know each other from a bunch of firms that push a stock. The most common manipulation—the one that the SEC is most involved with—is the so-called pump-and-dump scenario, where the brokers will get together, buy a lot of cheap stocks of a company, push it up with recommendations, unload it at the top, bet that the stock is going to go down, and then let it collapse. That's such a flagrant scenario it's quite obvious."

Some of the practices are uncanny, and purposefully beyond the understanding of mom-and-pop investors whose only interest is to sock away money into mutual funds for retirement. The following technique, called "death spiral financing," could hurt some investors with holdings of shares in small companies. Entrepreneurs who try to start up companies are sometimes targets of the practice.

Rothenberg lays out the scenario: "A company is so desperate for money that they get someone to finance them. As the financing fee they get stocks, and they get the stock based on certain price levels. In other words, the lower the stock goes, the more stock the partner who did the financing receives. So that partner has a tremendous incentive to sell short or get brokers to sell short and drive it down to get more stock. That's the death spiral. The theory is that the company ultimately will rebound. But by manipulating the stock down, the financing partner gets more stock. When the stock price snaps back, that partner can make a killing."

Even with the odds on Wall Street stacked against the individual investor, there are still sensible ways to invest, Rothenberg says.

He points to John Bogle as a guide. "He said you could do a lot worse than being 50 percent in a stock index fund and 50 percent in a bond index fund. That's as plain vanilla as you can get when your expenses are minimal. Vanguard and Fidelity charge the least. Fidelity has the Spartan fund, Vanguard has low-cost funds. As an alternative to that, and there's a reason to do this, you can be in Exchange Traded Fund—ETF—products. That way, you can buy the S&P 500 Stock Index, and you can buy a bond index."

ETFs have their advantages, he says. "The reason you would do an ETF fund rather than a stock fund is that when you buy into a stock or bond fund, you are buying internal capital gains. When they're distributed you don't get the benefit but you pay the taxes on it. With the ETF you pay capital gains on your own basis. So, it's also cost-efficient."

"If you're a long term investor, you have ten, fifteen, twenty, thirty year-time horizon, you want your expenses to be minimal, whether it's an ETF fund or a stock index fund. And basically you're going to ride through market cycles up and down—like we've been though the down cycle, now the up cycle. And you're in the market because of the long-term growth of the economy."

Consider an ETF (exchange traded fund). These make sense for individual investors.

Investors should consider having a higher percentage of their portfolio's overall asset allocation in international investments, he says.

"The growth rates abroad are much faster than the United States. I'm thinking particularly of China and India—and Brazil. Russia is a different problem because their legal system is worthless. The percentage of money internationally should be a lot higher than it used to be. It used to be 10 percent to 15 percent of an individual's portfolio. Now we're talking 30 percent or even more."

"That's simply because the growth rates of those countries are significantly higher than the United States. China may be the best example we can give, but understand if you are investing in Chinese securities, there's no legal system there that's worth anything. The reality is that the Chinese economy is growing at nine percent a year and ours is growing at one percent or maybe three percent if we really do a good job—but they're getting more than money influxes in an exports-driven economy. There's no problem with them pumping money into their economy."

A diverse allocation of assets will help balance investors' returns over the long term, he says. "The idea there is you don't want groups to go up and down together. Gold, for example, has gone up when the market was going down. So the concept of asset allocation, which is crucial to investment, is that you don't want to pick groups that overlap, and move the same way. In the long run, you're not benefiting from that."

Companies like Fidelity and Vanguard can explain this to investors in very simple terms so that they you can get adequately diversified, he says. "That way, you're not subject to everything collapsing at the same time."

If you are going to invest in individual stocks, be prepared for a wild ride, Rothenberg says. "The big stock I made a market in was Warner Communications before it merged with Time, and Southwest Airlines was another big stock. I had a stock—just to show you how crazy the market can be—called Charter Company. It was an oil trading company that also owned the Jacksonville National Bank. In the span of two years, the common stock went from $5 per share to $50 per share. A warrant (a security that allows the holder to buy stock at a specific price) went from one-eighth of a dollar, 12.5 cents, per share to $45 per share. And then back to zero. And then the common stock went from $5 per share to $50 per share to $2 per share in the span of eight months."

Charter Company did oil trading, he says. "In two years they were earning 50 cents a share and then two consecutive years they earn $14 a share and then $15 a share and then went back into the red."

"This was during the embargos—you know back in the seventies with the Shah and the revolution in Iran. With regard to Charter, one analyst, David Snow, who is now an independent energy and commodity expert, predicted it. He was a very aggressive buyer on the upside and he caught it right. But he was the only one. He was buying incredible quantities of stock. So from time to time an analyst can catch it right."

"I've had the experience of the wildest of stocks. But Warner went from $50 per share to $7 per share back to $50 per share. Then with the merger—the horrible merger with AOL announced in 2000—it collapsed. It was the worst merger in United States history." Rothenberg should know. His family's firm had been trading Warner stock since it was listed on the New York Stock Exchange in 1971.

"If investment returns are 91 percent asset allocation you shouldn't be in the business of picking stocks. There is no reason to believe that brokers or brokerage firms are any better. In fact, they're worse, because brokerage firms do underwriting for companies. They're biased."

Beware notorious penny stocks, says Rothenberg.

"Shares less than $5 are the definition of a penny stock. The SEC uses that definition, so the underwriters used to price their underwriting at $5, so it would not be a penny stock. The other ways to avoid [this designation] is if the company's shares are listed on NASDAQ or the New York [exchange], by definition it's not a penny stock."

One way to create such a penny stock company is by starting or acquiring a blank check company, he says. "This is a company that has no business other than raising money. And now they can invest it any way they want. And now, if they can get promoters to push the stock—there's no earnings, there's no anything. It's a blank check company. The promoters could be the individuals who control the company and/or affiliated brokers who are promoting the stock who get under the table stock or cash."

Rothenberg's former home away from home, the New York Stock Exchange, has lost plenty of power and prestige recently. Stock specialists and floor traders are disappearing fast. The New York Stock Exchange has lost much of the volume in stock trading, and therefore has lost much of its power and authority in the marketplace, Rothenberg argues.

"The market has changed a lot. As much as 75 percent of the trading now is fast money trading upstairs—the very quick arbitrage-related trading. The floor has lost all of its power. It's just a television show on that floor."

The new power on Wall Street is with fast money traders, Rothenberg contends. "You trade in microseconds—fractions of a second. You try to capture a one or two-cent spread back and forth as quickly as you can between markets. The New York Stock Exchange only does 30 percent of the volume in New York Stock

Exchange stocks now. NASDAQ has lost even more of its market share. You're talking about these dark pools. You've got a lot of stuff that's trading upstairs—that only their clients trade it."

The market for stocks is extremely fragmented now, he says. "You want the benefit of a central market. The small investor is only trading in the market that's exposed—the New York market or maybe NASDAQ. But if a majority are buying and trading away, and using these electronic platforms, the individual investor will never be exposed to that."

Another concern is to what extent this could be hurting the individual investor, he says. "We don't know what the pricing is or how much stock is traded and where." One danger facing investors is that the stock market has lost transparency, he says. "Now what do you have? You have a rigged game, and who wants to play in a rigged game? I think that's pretty serious."

The large buy-side institutions like pension funds and mutual funds use their own research analysts and don't rely on Wall Street, he says.

The market downturn starting in 2007 did not catch Rothenberg unawares or by surprise. "I was expecting it. Absolutely. We sold our house when the market started to soften in real estate, back in 2006. We knew about all these interest-only mortgage loans, adjustable-rate mortgage loans. We knew that if the real estate market crashed, the underlying mortgages would crash, which means the financial institutions would crash, along with all of the derivative markets. There were hedge fund [investors] who cleaned up because they understood that the fundamentals of the economy would work their way through the entire financial system, bankrupting banks and brokers along the way, and customers owning their products. No one has figured out how to prevent cycles in the economy. It doesn't look like they're going to figure it out, either. Underlying the fickle economy is the fickle nature of the stock market."

While the residential real estate market has crashed, Rothenberg and many others are watching the commercial real estate market for a potential disaster.

"The commercial loan side has just started to crash. Empty malls are all over the country, trying to find refinancing. They have terribly bad underwriting practices on the commercial side. Will there be a double dip recession? Are the banks reserving enough on the commercial side for the second dip?"

Lessons & Takeaways

- We all fall in love with our stocks, but remember, they don't love us back. When buying and selling stocks, make an objective and informed decision devoid of emotion.
- Avoid small company stocks that are thinly traded and easy to maniplate. Stick with large-capitalization stocks of well-known companies.
- Large institutions have gained tremendous influence on Wall Street.
- Regulators often do not understand new and complex trading methods.
- Beware of penny stocks, meaning stocks that trade for $5 or less. Financial serial killers know how to manipulate the share price of these small companies.

CHAPTER
THIRTEEN

The Consequence of White-Collar Crime and How It Can Destroy Lives and Rip Families Apart

Tom Barden was a special agent in the New York Office of the FBI for twenty-one years. He specialized in investigating a variety of white-collar crimes, including the WorldCom accounting fraud case and several other high-profile investigations. Barden's final assignment was as an assistant special agent in charge of the white-collar crime branch of the New York Office of the FBI. He was essentially the number-two guy for the FBI in New York investigating white-collar crime and financial serial killers.

Financial serial killers frequently push buttons related to core elements of our personality, including masculinity and family, Barden says.

"I think [victims] often want to be successful; they want to feel good about themselves. They run in circles with other people who are 'successful' and they want to feel like that. They want to be like the guy—you know at the country club—who brags about some sort of big score he made, whether he made one or not."

The man of the house doesn't want to be shamed, Barden says. Financial serial killers understand how to appeal to the male psyche and play upon fears of inadequacy. The victim "doesn't want to feel that they won't take a chance. He really wants to feel like he has the authority to say, 'Okay, this sounds like a good stock deal. I'll take a chance for two bucks a share.' If the mark responded, 'Yeah, I'll check with my wife,' the con artist would say, 'Come on, what kind of man are you?'"

The financial serial killer would not insult the victim, or ask that question "in a nasty way," Barden says. The victim at that point could hang up the phone. The tone was more jocular. "'Come on, you're the man of your house, you can make this decision,'" recounts Barden, who made hundreds of investigations into such scams. "'It's only two bucks a share.' That's playing on their masculinity."

"People should be leery of, and I hate to say it, the family member who says that the opportunity is just too good to be true," Barden says. "Whether it is a scam or whether it is something legitimate, you don't want to say no to a family member. That relationship can put you in a bind."

Stay away from the relationships. Find an objective adviser who is not a family member with whom you don't have some emotional ties. "When you and the adviser have a very strict business relationship, there is less of an emotional conflict, and it's easier to say no to an investment idea or opportunity."

Greed is far from the only factor that motivates people when they meet a financial serial killer. Desperation is also extremely significant. "I have witnessed several cases that, when someone becomes a victim, he is at a point in his life when he is really just down on his luck. And he wants to find an opportunity to get out of where he is."

John Moscow recalls one case involving a financial serial killer who sold merchants goods on consignment. They included diamonds, clothes, or other items. After he sold the merchants' goods, he refused to pay them the money he got from selling their items. He simply swindled those merchants. He'd make one down payment for the goods, but refused to pay the rest. "He thought that by making this one small initial payment he could somehow avoid a criminal complaint being made against him. Then he used mob muscle to keep the merchants from trying to get their goods back," recalls Moscow.

"You would have families where one day they were middle-class families—making a little profit every day on what they sold from the goods, whether it was furs or clothes or diamonds, what have you—and the next day they were broke. They were in debt. They had no assets. They had nothing to turnover and sell. They had to get the kids out of college and reach into whatever retirement or investment funds they had. They were totally destroyed. And that particular guy enjoyed seeing it."

"The harm to the victims was just incredible. By victims I don't just mean each merchant who was swindled, but I also mean his wife, his children, their relatives. The family was destroyed. They went from functioning and well-off to totally broke. Sometimes the swindler would make a devil's bargain, offering the merchant enough of his stuff back so that he could struggle to continue to exist, on the understanding that he would act as a reference for the good faith of the man who had swindled him. That's pretty vicious stuff."

One of Moscow's major cases was a large bank fraud. Again, it involved merchants who had their accounts at a bank that then failed. This particular bank, the Bank of Credit and Commerce

International, had hundreds of thousands of depositors. Moscow says "the big losers were the merchants. By merchants I mean people who were buying goods and selling them in a store, anyone who had a commercial establishment with a bank account. There were hundreds of thousands of them. If you take all their money from them, you destroy them. Then the neighborhood has to do without the goods and services that the merchants would have provided. They were people who put money into the bank so that they could pay their estimated taxes. When the bank went under, they still had to pay their taxes; they just didn't have the money."

"Another consequence is that each landlord for each merchant is now faced with less income or they need to raise the rent on the remaining tenants. The community might lose its food store; the community then needs another store."

Moscow is currently working with the bankruptcy trustee assigned to recover money for the victims of the Bernie Madoff fraud.

Moscow says "the Madoff scheme involved an investment with an incredibly high success rate, moderate returns—high but moderate returns—but totally fictitious numbers. And a totally fictitious course of behavior. No transparency. Madoff would tell new investors, 'We can't let you invest. This is too exclusive, you can't be allowed in.' By making it clear that people would not be allowed in, it made it sound desirable so that people would want to invest. Financially it looked like a really good deal. But it was all bogus. The money was all stolen."

"As far as I know, the scheme started no later than 1962. There is an argument that maybe it started in 1961. At the moment, we're talking about something that lasted forty-six years. A very, very long time. When it collapsed, people who had put their life savings in with Madoff went from having money to not having money."

"We have been told stories by a number of different women who said that Madoff went to them when they were just divorced and persuaded them to put all of their alimony settlement or divorce settlement in with him. We have a woman who was living in the nicest neighborhood of New York City, with an expensive car, and she thought she had money in the bank, the interest on which would support her lifestyle. All of a sudden she has no money in the bank, but she still has to pay for the car, she still has to pay for the apartment, and you know, she might now and again sometimes want to eat. Money's all gone. She's an older woman. She can't earn any money. It's gone."

"What do you do when a nursing home calls, and says, 'Look you have a ninety-two-year-old woman here. She isn't a charity case. We can't keep her. If you don't pay the bill, we're going to have to throw her out. All of her money was with Madoff.'"

The carnage and damage from Madoff seems to go on forever. Moscow estimates that there are at least 8,000 victims, both individuals and investment funds. It's the people—the real live human beings—who continue to suffer. "We know that there are people who have to sell their houses, and have to sell their cars. Their standard of living drops. We know that there are people who just disappear from their usual haunts where they used to be with their friends. They just can't afford to go to these places anymore."

"It takes a certain amount of detachment to note the costs and yet not get involved in the individual lives of the people who are suffering. In my experience, these victims' demand for emotional support is infinite. There is no financial or emotional support that is really worthwhile that I can provide or that my colleagues can provide, except to try to recover their money and get something to these people so that they are not out on the streets or eating cat food."

In the Madoff case there have even been some suicides. Moscow recounts a couple of stories. "People committed suicide because of the loss of the money. One out of England—an army veteran—who actually put money into Madoff and was sufficiently shamed in his eyes—dishonored—so he killed himself."

People who lose their money often lose their homes. When they lose their homes, they are no longer in their neighborhood with their friends. So they lose that support system. Plus, when you lose your home and leave the neighborhood, you often have to pull your children out of school. Many people move in with family or friends who don't live in the school district where the victim's children had been attending school. This type of disruption to normal family life causes stress in many marriages, some of which will end in divorce.

Once you lose your money from a fraud, you don't have a nest egg to protect yourself from emergencies in life, such as the loss of a job or unexpected medical bills. In Moscow's eyes, financial fraud "is a far more vicious crime in my view than the robbery that takes from you everything that you have on your body. People don't carry their worldly goods around with them. If a cleaning lady has her day's wages [on] her and then somebody pulls a knife on her she will lose only the money she has with her at that time. Yet in a financial fraud the thief is stealing from her not just that day's wages but a whole lot more. He has taken her savings, which could be many days or years of her wages. The financial con man may also be putting her in debt because she does not have enough cash, she has no cash reserves left. Now she can't buy food or pay her rent.

"No armed robber can steal a pension fund. No armed robber can steal a retirement fund. No armed robber can effectively steal the title to your home. Swindlers can, and they do."

"The big losers are people who trust other people to handle their money, and the big losses come with money that is entrusted to the care of others. People who commit robberies may cause physical injury, and they create fear, but they cannot begin to cause the financial catastrophes of totally destroying a family economically."

Moscow saw many cases when he worked in the Manhattan district attorney's office where victims of financial fraud had to borrow money and then got in debt. The people lending have a risk of nonpayment so they charge enough so that they break even and make some profit. "And whether they are loan sharks using violence or merely high-interest-rate lenders who are in fact pricing their loans fairly, interest rates are still going to be very high. And the poor folks who are robbed can't afford that."

"The costs of a financial crime are not just what the con man took, but the impact on the lives of the people from whom he took it. If you take someone who is saving $10 a week on an income of $500 a week and you steal $100 from them, have you stolen that day's wages or have you stolen ten weeks' savings? Have you put them in debt? Have you destroyed the possibility of their kids having a birthday party? Whatever it is, there are collateral damages from the theft."

"When you start getting into the bigger money losses, of course, people have to sell their homes. There's nothing else to be done. They have to move. Their kids have to move. The friendships are broken. Frequently what you find is that, because people don't have money, they can't do the things that their friends are doing and they lose their friends. These are all collateral consequences of the swindle. And you have more immediate domestic consequences when a husband tells his wife that instead of being rich they're broke. The family has a house note, car note, and other financial obligations that oblige him to pay more money than they have. Now you have a marriage that is in trouble."

"The impact on families can be dramatic. I've seen it. For most marriages money is a major factor. If the husband has to tell the wife, or the wife has to tell the husband, that their home is at risk, their economy is destroyed, and their position economically in the world has been completely altered by what happened yesterday, that's going to have a dreadful impact on the family, on the marriage, and on their future, if any exists. It just does. Even if the husband goes away looking somewhere else for a job, the wife has to go out looking for a job. The kids, for whom mom stayed home to care, are now uncared for. Think about it, these are all understandable collateral consequences of the decline of family fortunes that had not been planned. This is a catastrophic end to a lifestyle that was supportable and now has become way out of their league."

Moscow recalls another case where he was dealing with a "particularly vile broker" who called a man he knew and tried to get him to invest. "But the man was in the hospital and the wife answered the phone. He tries to persuade the wife to mortgage the house that they were living in so that they could invest in the phony stocks that the broker was selling. The broker knew the husband was sick, and he knew they were in financial trouble, but he tried to get the wife to mortgage the house to raise some money so that he could go out and spend it on strippers and cocaine, with some vodka and some champagne on top. It was, as I said, vile. To this broker that was the sort of thing that he thought was good fun."

Continuing to go after the helpless, this broker and his friends found another victim, a man who drank in the afternoon. "They would call him in the afternoon with business deals. So he lost $18 million in one deal, $10 million in another. He had spent a long time building up a fortune in the food additives business and he thought because he was rich that he was smart, and it just wasn't so. He was a really good guy in the food additives business, but didn't know anything about finance."

The financial serial killer must be emotionally detached from what he is doing, Moscow concludes, "because, quite frankly, a rational, nonemotional description of the conduct of the people involved has an awfully chilling sound when somebody hears it."

Here's a story about a one-time leading Wall Street firm and how its brokers drove one client to contemplate suicide.

The Singh family had accumulated a fortune of $20 million partly derived from income from a family business in India and partly through investments of the family's business income. They entrusted their entire fortune to Prudential Securities in New York. Within eight months of receiving the money, Prudential lost it all.

Singh originally handled the family's fortune himself. He used a discount brokerage and made his own investment decisions. Some of the family money was in a trust account, some in a joint account held by him and his wife, and the rest was in two trust accounts for his young children.

One day in July 1997 Singh was standing in line at his discount brokerage firm when he began talking to another customer. The customer was of Indian descent, as was Singh. They spoke to one another in their native tongue. Singh confided to this man that the family accounts had not performed very well the last year and he was coming to realize that the family would benefit from the advice of a professional money manager.

The man standing in line told Singh that his cousin, also Indian, was a successful broker with a well-known firm. Singh listened intently to stories of how this man's cousin had invested prudently and wisely for his customers. Singh took down the broker's name and phone number, and made an appointment to see him.

The meeting went well and Singh transferred all of the family's money to the care of the broker. The broker managed the money well. It didn't hurt that the broker was investing the money during the late 1990s, when the bull market was in full swing. The stock market was heading higher and higher each day. Millions of investors saw their savings head toward the moon, as did Singh.

At the end of 1999, Singh's broker decided to move to Prudential Securities. He convinced Singh to permit him to take the family account along. The broker assured Singh that Prudential was a very reputable firm, well managed, and "solid as a rock." Singh agreed to follow his broker.

What the broker never told Singh was that the broker and his assistant were personally paid a $1 million bonus for moving the Singh family accounts, and the brokers' other accounts, to Prudential. So the move to Prudential was not really done for the benefit of Singh and the other customers, but instead was for the personal financial benefit of the broker. (This is quite common—veteran brokers are offered astronomical sums to leave one firm and join another. At this writing, major Wall Street firms are offering veteran stockbrokers packages that could pay up to 330 percent of their last year's fees and commissions to move. Imagine that. That's more than three years' pay to leave one firm and join another.)

At the beginning of 2000 the broker began to furiously trade stocks and options in the Singh family accounts. There appeared to be no rhyme or reason to the trading. All that can be said was that the trading was frequent and mostly in technology and telecommunication stocks. When the stocks fell, the broker loaded up on more of them, convinced that they were a bargain. The stocks continued to fall in value. The broker also filled the accounts with options to purchase and sell stocks, but his timing was awful. The accounts plummeted in value. After a few short months, the Singh family was completely wiped out. All that was left of their $20 million fortune was $100,000!

Singh was in a state of shock. He was confused, bewildered, and stunned. When he had agreed to let the broker move his accounts to Prudential, just a few months previously, he had been treated like a king. The broker had introduced Singh to the

manager of the Prudential branch. The manager had taken Singh
into his well-appointed office, welcomed Singh to the firm, and
treated him like a long-lost family member. Singh was made to
feel special. He was important to Prudential, a very valued client,
the branch manager said.

After Singh's money had been lost in the casino called
Prudential, Singh was an outcast. No one would return his calls.
He was ushered out the door and left to fend for himself. The
king was now a mere peasant.

Singh retreated to his home. He was ashamed of himself, even
though none of this was his fault. He had entrusted his money
to his broker and Prudential. He had even agreed to the firm's
request that he hand over complete discretion to Prudential to
manage the money. Singh had signed the formal discretionary
account agreement that Prudential slipped across the desk to
him. This form guaranteed that Prudential would have complete
discretion to manage the Singhs' savings as Prudential saw fit, in
its professional judgment.

Singh fell into a deep depression and seriously contemplated
suicide. Each day for an entire year he beat himself up over the
debacle. During that year, he slept on the couch in his living room,
unable to sleep in the same bed as his wife. The thought swirled
in his head that maybe, yes, maybe, he did deserve to die.

Lessons & Takeaways

- Losing your savings will take an emotional and physical toll on you and your loved ones. Get serious about investing your money and protecting it.
- We are all living longer so our money has to last longer. Guard your savings extremely carefully.
- When you lose money, you are not just losing paper bills. You may also lose your home, your car, and other items you need to live. Your ability to pay for your children's schooling will be jeopardized. You may not have the money you need in case of a medical emergency. This is serious business, so continue to educate yourself. You've taken the first step by reading this book.
- If you are the victim of a financial fraud or swindle, or lose your money in a bad investment, you will suffer mentally and emotionally. Don't be afraid to seek professional counseling.

CHAPTER
FOURTEEN

Web Tools and Databases
to Spot Trouble Before It Starts

After Bernie Madoff revealed himself to be a thief, newspapers and magazines routinely ran lists of organizations and Web sites investors could turn to for information about their broker or adviser. Investors were scared, wanted to make sure of their advisers' credibility, and needed information to do so.

When Madoff confessed his crimes, investors across America must have had the same chilling thought: Good lord, is my broker/adviser a crook, too? (In fact, a stockbroker confessed to coauthor Bruce Kelly that he wished he had a book *just like this one* to hand his clients in order to calm their fears. Remember, clients were dealing with fears about their broker/adviser during a historic stock market collapse of 2008 and 2009, so investors needed a tremendous amount of reassuring from their financial professionals at the time.)

Another inspiration to write this book developed from the fact that the lists in newspapers and magazines, while timely, are lacking. They simply aren't enough to educate investors to the risks they face. People don't learn from reading lists; they learn from reading stories. That's why we filled this book with true tales of financial serial killers. A list in a newspaper or magazine is a good reference, but after it's posted on the fridge and then covered over with vacation pictures or kids' artwork, it's forgotten. That said, lists do have value—they are handy, concise, and easy to use. So, here is our list of references, drawn from our experiences as well as a couple of short articles from national publications that will help you detect con men and protect your savings.

First, do a simple Google check of the broker or adviser. This may sound simplistic, but it is worthwhile.

Second, FINRA has a good database that provides background information about each registered stockbroker. (It can be found at FINRA's Web site, www.FINRA.org.) It's called BrokerCheck, and if investors click on the label designated for them on the main page, the FINRA BrokerCheck tab is on the right-hand side of the next screen under the "most viewed" column.

BrokerCheck has background information on 850,000 brokers and 17,000 securities firms currently or formerly registered with FINRA. It includes information about previous employment, histories of any disciplinary problems, and customer complaints. The system at times is a little difficult to use if the broker has a very common name such as John Smith. There are many John Smiths, so you have to use the advanced search function and include the name of his brokerage firm as part of the search request.

Financial serial killers often get their start in the brokerage business and then are fired, and obviously they don't want you to find out about that. So they will use a name on their business card that doesn't match their name in the FINRA database. Or they will drop their first name and use their middle name, add an initial, subtract a hyphen, or create a slight oddity of spelling so their record is obscured. So, be careful about that.

Using BrokerCheck, you can also check up on the brokerage firm your adviser works with. This is very telling. This lists any fines, lawsuits, or compliance problems the firm has had in its past. If the firm has an abundance of problems, know that before handing your money over to one of its brokers.

Third, for information on investment advisers who are not registered with FINRA, investors can only check out the investment advisory firm with the Securities and Exchange Commission (www.adviserinfo.sec.gov). This is the Investment Adviser Public Disclosure Web site, and it gives background information about the investment advisory firms regulated by the SEC and the states. It provides a "Form ADV," a disclosure document required by the SEC that reveals lawsuits, fines, suspensions, or other sanctions involving the firm.

Fourth, state regulators also keep records of brokers licensed in their state. On the Web, go to www.nasaa.org for the site of an organization called the North American Securities Administrators Association. Contact information for each state regulator is on the site. Call up the press or public information officer and ask for information about your broker. State regulators often keep more complete files on brokers than FINRA does, and they can e-mail you a file with the broker's employment history.

Fifth, the CFP Board, which controls the certified financial planning credential, keeps records of disciplinary actions and ethics complaints against any financial planner. Information on individuals registered with the CFP Board, as well as their disciplinary history, is available on the CFP Board's Web site, www.cfp.net. A search tool for the database is located on the Web site's home page.

CHAPTER
FIFTEEN

Four Outlandish Tales of the Securities Business

The securities and investment advice businesses are like any other, say the furniture industry. They employ highly-trained and talented people, as well as those who come up way short. The difference, of course, between a furniture company and a financial services company is the stakes. You're not just buying a sofa, but need to protect your life savings. Before handing your money to a broker or an investment adviser, beware.

In this chapter, we tell four brief stories of the bad, sad and ugly in the investment advice and securities industries. Taken from the pages of *InvestmentNews*, the first three stories show the investment advice business employs potentially dangerous, unstable and unethical people. Does the securities business look to hire such individuals? Of course not. However, these tales show that financial serial killers can come in many guises.

The final story, about an Iraq war veteran who returned home hoping to restart his career as a stock broker, is not about a financial serial killer. Instead, it shows the disregard that a large institution may have for an employee who happens to be in charge of millions of dollars of clients' money.

One stockbroker who was kicked out of the securities business for monkeying around with a client's money found a new calling: local politics. In November 2009, the ex-broker, Kevin O'Brien, was elected to public office in a Cincinnati suburb where he became one of three officials in charge of the town's annual budget of $35 million.

Two months earlier, in September 2009, FINRA permanently barred O'Brien from working in the securities industry in any capacity. O'Brien, until 2008 a broker in Cincinnati with Robert W. Baird & Co., misappropriated client funds for his own benefit when he transferred $378,000 between client accounts, according to FINRA records.

According to a letter from FINRA regulators that outlines O'Brien's settlement, he used a portion of the $378,000 to pay for legitimate expenses on behalf of the client. He misappropriated the rest "by writing checks to himself and to a charitable organization for which he was treasurer, and by withdrawing cash using an ATM card."

O'Brien is a director of the Children's Rights Council, a nonprofit organization that serves divorced, never married, and extended families, according to its Web site. It wasn't clear if that was the charity named in the letter.

As is standard in the securities business, O'Brien agreed to the ban without admitting or denying any of the findings. His former firm, Baird, reimbursed the client $285,000. It's common in the securities business to have such matters settled quietly.

Having run for local office in Ohio a number of times over the years, O'Brien once again turned to municipal politics and in November won election as an Anderson Township trustee, garnering 6,018 votes—second-highest in a field of five candidates.

With a population of 43,500, Anderson has three trustees who manage the town's finances and oversee its fire and police departments, and payments for roads. The position pays about $19,000 a year. O'Brien's record in the securities business was not an election issue, some residents say, because it came to light after the election. One of the banned broker's campaign slogans was "integrity counts," the residents added.

Townspeople are "outraged and embarrassed," says Peggy Reis, a trustee who won reelection in November.

Although most swearing-in ceremonies are public affairs, O'Brien was sworn in privately about six weeks after the election.

According to FINRA records, O'Brien engaged in outside business activities for his clients but did not inform Baird about them. He made the transfer of money between accounts while engaging in those activities for clients, FINRA said.

Also according to FINRA records, it was the second time O'Brien had drawn scrutiny for such outside business activities. In most cases, that means the broker sold investments or made transactions off the radar of his firm.

Although FINRA has kicked him out of the securities business, O'Brien still works in the financial advice arena, operating his own financial consulting business, O'Brien Private Wealth Management. That firm, however, is not listed in the Securities and Exchange Commission's database of financial advisory firms. O'Brien stressed that he voluntarily gave up his FINRA license to "devote time and energy to other businesses." Along with the wealth management firm, he runs a company that designs and hosts Web sites. When asked what O'Brien Private Wealth Management does, he said that the firm has private clients and is "being very careful not to violate terms with FINRA."

He would not specifically say what type of investment products the firm is involved with or discuss in detail its services. The Web site, however, lists "research of individual stock, bond and investment issues" as one of its services. In April 2010, O'Brien was sued by Baird for $344,000, roughly the amount he allegedly stole. So goes the securities business.

A former investment adviser who once told the Internal Revenue Service that he had "citizenship in heaven"—and not the United States—was sentenced in a federal court in Dallas in September 2009 to forty months in prison for setting up a series of sham offshore investments that worked as tax dodges. According to a statement from the Department of Justice, the ex-adviser and estate planner, Lanas Evans Troxler, operated a series of tax and financial-advice businesses from at least 1998 to 2002.

Beginning in 1997, Troxler set up a series of offshore businesses in the Turks and Caicos Islands for himself and his clients and also steered his clients to accountants who prepared phony tax returns, the Justice Department said. He used the offshore businesses to make it appear as if his clients had made certain transactions that created income that should have been, but was not, reported on federal individual and business income tax returns.

In 2008, he was convicted of one count of obstructing IRS laws, four counts of attempting tax evasion, and twelve counts of assisting in the preparation of false tax returns. The resulting

IRS tax loss was more than $630,000. As part of his sentence, he was ordered to pay a fine of $10,000.

When working as an adviser, Troxler in 2002 told the IRS that he was not a U.S. citizen but rather a "child of God," and therefore his citizenship was "in heaven," according to documents released by the Justice Department.

Troxler had other ideas about his residency. He also reportedly told the IRS that he was an inhabitant of Texas, a republic established by a Spanish Land Grant.

A Tennessee broker formerly affiliated with the firm AIG Financial Advisors Inc. spent time making voodoo dolls of his victims to ward off their damaging testimony, prosecutors said.

Barry R. Stokes pleaded guilty in 2008 to multiple counts of embezzlement, as well as mail and wire fraud and money laundering for stealing $19 million from some 35,000 victims nationwide, according to the U.S. Attorney's Office in Nashville, Tennessee. The theft came from clients' 401(k), health savings, and dependent care accounts. His firm, 1 Point Solutions, was an employee benefits administration company based in Dickson, Tennessee.

Stokes was registered with AIG Financial Advisors from October 2005 to September 2006, at which point his fraud was discovered and he was fired, according to brokerage records on file with the states where he was licensed to do business.

In September 2009, Stokes was sentenced in federal court in Nashville to twelve years in prison after a hearing that presented evidence of his bizarre practices. At a presentencing hearing, prosecutors also said that Stokes paid a psychic with a credit card to give him readings while in jail. He also wrote a letter to the psychic saying that he was lighting candles and throwing salt over his shoulder to keep critics and creditors at bay.

A stockbroker returns to the securities business after being injured in the Iraq war, only to discover his firm has taken his clients and is suing him over a pay dispute.

Wall Street and the investment business sometimes treat its own incredibly poorly. Keep that in mind when you are handing over your life savings to a broker or investment adviser. If a broker's firm is harassing him, how will he focus on you and your money?

As a corporal in the Marine Corps Reserves, Jay Belanger was sent into action during the U.S. invasion of Iraq in March 2003.

The convoy gunner's unit was attacked on a desert highway 100 miles southwest of Baghdad, about two weeks after the war began. The wounds he suffered in the attack left him with facial scars and permanent hearing loss in both ears.

After being treated for his injuries, he rejoined his unit and was promoted to sergeant. Later that year, Belanger was discharged and went back home to Connecticut. In December 2003, he contacted his boss about getting his old job back as a representative for Prudential Securities.

According to a lawsuit filed in December 2009 in U.S. District Court for the District of Connecticut, that conversation did not go well. Before he went to Iraq, Belanger had a book of business that, at the top of the bull market in 2000, had 150 accounts and $11 million in assets, earning him an income of about $100,000 a year. While he was gone, Prudential Securities Inc. merged with Wachovia Securities. According to the lawsuit, the branch manager told him that his customers had been given to other representatives. Instead, Belanger, who also fought in the Gulf War, was offered a position as a broker in a Wachovia bank branch, with an annual salary of $44,000 and minimal commissions. He worked in the job for a few months before resigning.

Belanger's suit alleges that Wachovia, its successor Wells Fargo Advisors, and predecessor, Prudential Securities, violated his rights under the Uniformed Services Employment and Reemployment Rights Act (USERRA) of 1994. That law requires employers to protect employees' careers while they are on active military duty. Belanger's suit claims that Wachovia and its related firms "systematically destroyed his client base and book of business."

It was the second time in 2009 that Wachovia has confronted charges that it violated the law and harmed the livelihoods of brokers when they returned from serving in the military. In March, a judge awarded veteran and broker Michael Serricchio close to $1 million in back pay, damages, and legal fees after he won a lawsuit against Wachovia in a trial in federal court in Connecticut. He was reinstated to his job at Wells Fargo Advisors and he was guaranteed a monthly salary of $12,300 for one year. Like Belanger, Serricchio was a broker with Prudential Securities before Wachovia bought a majority stake of the brokerage in 2003. His lawsuit claimed that when he returned from the Air Force in 2003, he was offered a reduced position, his accounts were gone, and he was told he would have to rebuild his book of business.

Teresa Dougherty, a Wells Fargo Advisors spokesperson said that Wachovia has been recognized for its exemplary treatment of military personnel. In 2005, "Wachovia was awarded the

Employer Support for Freedom Award from the U.S. Secretary of Defense in recognition of our policies and practices with regard to treatment of employees on military leave," she said.

Belanger and Serricchio aren't alone, according to one lawyer who specializes in USERRA claims. He said that the securities industry has violated the rights of many brokers and bankers who have returned home from active military duty only to find their old jobs and salaries gone.

"This is not something that's unusual," said Mat Tully, founding partner with Tully Rinckey PLLC. He said that his firm is working on "two hundred active cases" involving Wall Street firms. Since the terrorist attacks of September 11, 2001, "we're seeing people [on Wall Street] being fired because of military deployment." Part of the problem is the nature of the brokerage business. "The Wall Street industry is unique," because pay for brokers and advisers is earned through relationships with clients and by building a book of business. When reps and bankers are deployed overseas, some repeatedly, their absence can fray nerves of clients and employers. When a broker leaves for military service, his clients are handed off to other brokers to tend and maintain until the rep returns. Some clients don't like moving back and forth between brokers. "When you come back from war, how do you reconstruct the book of business?"

Wall Street firms often would rather settle lawsuits involving veterans rather than risking the publicity of taking a case to trial. Under USERRA, claimants can usually sue and receive compensatory damages, or what they were owed in back pay. Tully thinks that the law lacks teeth because claimants typically have great difficulty getting punitive damages, which are more common in other kinds of discrimination claims. That only emboldens Wall Street firms to act negligently when veterans return, he said.

Belanger, who remained in the business and is now affiliated with LPL Financial, uses a hearing aid to compensate for his war injuries.

According to Belanger's lawsuit, Wachovia sued him in 2009, filing a FINRA arbitration claim to collect about $30,000. That was the balance from a forgivable note. Brokerage firms give recruits such notes or loans as an enticement to leave one firm and join a new firm. Belanger was given such a loan, to be worked off over time, when he first joined Prudential Securities in 2000, his attorney, Thomas Willcutts, said. Belanger's manager informally told him to forget about repaying the loan when he left the firm, Willcutts said.

Wachovia was allegedly quite aggressive about getting its $30,000 from the war veteran, Willcutts said. Wachovia "had a collections outfit out of New Jersey." On the collection agency's Web site, it boasted about "using creative techniques," to get its money back, Willcutts said.

CHAPTER
SIXTEEN

Elder Abuse and Fraud

Elder abuse can happen to any family, even the high and mighty. Take the case of deceased heiress Brooke Astor.

In 2009, Anthony Marshall, Mrs. Astor's son, and attorney Francis X. Morrissey were both sentenced to a state prison term of one to three years for defrauding and stealing from the legendary philanthropist.

Elder abuse is a term referring to any knowing, intentional, or negligent act by a caregiver or any other person that causes harm or a serious risk of harm to a vulnerable adult. The specificity of laws varies from state to state, but broadly defined, abuse ranges from physical violence to emotional abuse. Elder abuse can include inflicting mental pain, anguish, or distress on an elder person through verbal or nonverbal acts. It includes neglect and abandonment, as well. We are going to focus on issues involving relationships and money—the illegal taking, misuse, or concealment of funds, property, or assets of a vulnerable elder.

Indicators of emotional abuse may include an unexplained withdrawal from normal activities, a sudden change in alertness, or unusual depression. Sudden changes in financial situations may be the result of exploitation. Not only are they often lonely, many older people begin to lose their ability to make sound decisions and often listen to the last person they speak to, as Lillian Wentz did when she sold her $24 million of Berkshire Hathaway stock.

The elderly are truly the most vulnerable to financial serial killers—this book is for them. We also hope that adult children whose parents are retired in Florida, Arizona, or in other sunny climes take notice of this book, too. Too often, regulators and prosecutors uncover stories of financial serial killers preying on groups of older people who live in retirement communities.

Television networks used to ask, *It's ten o'clock. Do you know where your children are?*

We're asking, *It's twelve noon. Do you know who's treating your mother to a free lunch in Florida to talk about investments with spectacular, market-beating "guaranteed" returns?*

The SEC knows that elderly people are targeted by financial serial killers and need to be protected from the con artists of the financial industry. The agency has issued a report specifically addressing the risks associated with "free-lunch" sales seminars. The agency conducted an investigation into 110 firms that offer these events. It then reported that many seminars are specifically designed to solicit seniors, advertised as educational events, with names like "Seniors Financial Survival Seminar" or "Senior Financial Safety Workshop." Seniors are promised "free" advice by "experts" on subjects ranging from attaining a secure retirement, to financial planning, to inheritance advice.

In addition to offering these dine-and-learn seminars in attractive, upscale locales, the seminar sponsors frequently use other incentives such as door prizes and vacations to encourage attendance. The SEC warns in its report that sponsors often use typical high-pressure sales tactics that convey a sense of urgency, such as "limited seating available," or "call *now* to reserve a seat."

Misleading and exaggerated statements on seminar mailers and advertisements were found in half of the SEC's examinations of the brokerage firms. Firms made outrageous claims such as "Immediately add $100,000 to your net worth," "How to receive a 13.3 percent return," and "How $100K can pay one Million to Your Heirs." The SEC also found seminar materials often failed to disclose critical information, and warned that attendees may not understand that the seminar would be sponsored by an undisclosed company with a financial interest in product sales.

Not surprisingly, the agency found that 59 percent of the firms offering the "free-lunch" seminars had inadequate supervisory procedures in place. In twenty-five of the examinations, the agency found that unsuitable recommendations had been made to the investor, either at the seminar or after the attendee opened an account. In fourteen examinations, the agency found evidence of serious misrepresentations and possible outright fraud. Those firms who were in violation received "deficiency letters" or "letters of caution," and the report recommended that financial services firms "should take steps to supervise sales seminars more closely."

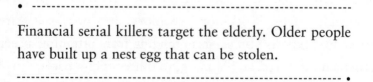

Financial serial killers target the elderly. Older people have built up a nest egg that can be stolen.

Families will always fight about money; now, in a time of deep economic distress, the battles can get uglier.

Beware of one family member suddenly cozying up to an older relative, says former FBI agent Tom Barden. "There are examples where relatives come in and pay the bills, take them to the movies, and act as a companion for the older person," Barden says. "I think children of those elder parents should also be leery of Uncle Bill, who all of a sudden happens to move down to where Mom and Dad are living, and he starts to hang around quite a bit.

"The message is to the elderly people—be wary of that sibling or that son or daughter, sister or brother that is looking to be the person to protect your assets. You almost need to have two people to be custodians. That way you have checks and balances. That way there will be no dispute, because people are going to call up Mom and say *Mom, you know I just lost my job and I lost my house and I need to borrow a few thousand dollars.*"

Sometimes, it's not family members who damage an elderly person. It's a stockbroker or investment adviser.

One recent securities arbitration case focused on the abuse of an older person. In an extreme rarity for the securities business, an arbitrator in December 2009 cited elder abuse when tripling the damages a discount securities firm must pay a ninety-six-year-old client.

A FINRA panel awarded the elderly investor, David Wolfson, $1.6 million in a case involving StockCross Financial Services Inc. of Beverly Hills, California.

Wolfson accused StockCross, along with two of its brokers, of misconduct and self-dealing. He claimed the brokers recommended and solicited unsuitable and overly risky investments that were actively traded on margin. The claim also alleged that StockCross and the two brokers, Thomas B. Cooper and Peter L. Boorn, put Wolfson's home at risk. Wolfson was a client of Cooper for decades. According to the complaint, they "encouraged and invited Mr. Wolfson to leverage the equity in his home with a reverse-mortgage transaction to utilize as investment capital."

A footnote to the lawsuit alleged that Cooper "quit because he had bilked nearly all of Mr. Wolfson's assets—including the equity in his home, all his cash reserves, all his emergency/medical cash reserves, and even the insurance money Mr. Wolfson received to replace his automobile—and there was nothing left to churn."

The arbitrators awarded Wolfson $320,000 in compensatory damages and $960,000 in damages for elder abuse. They also awarded the ninety-six-year-old $234,000 in legal fees, expert witness fees of $62,000, and various costs of $21,000 and $10,000 as sanctions for failing to follow discovery orders.

StockCross and the brokers will fight the decision and file a motion to vacate, said Martin H. Kaplan, the attorney filing the motion. Such motions to vacate are essentially court appeals of FINRA arbitration awards, which are very difficult to overturn.

Kaplan, a partner with Gusrae, Kaplan, Bruno & Nusbaum PLLC, said the arbitration panel "exceeded its authority" in the matter and its decision against StockCross showed a bias because of its detailed discussion of the discovery process.

While many arbitration claims charge elder abuse, it is extremely rare for a FINRA panel to cite such abuse in an award, says David Liebrader, an attorney that represents both investors and brokers against securities firms. Under California law, elder abuse entitles plaintiffs to triple the damages.

The three arbitrators in the Wolfson case took into consideration his attorney's argument for punitive damages and elder abuse.

The legal brief arguing for damages is sad and distressing reading. "At the core of this case is a trusting, elderly widowed man at ninety-six years of age named David Wolfson. Wolfson was a high school dropout and possessed no formal education. Wolfson was legally disabled and in ill health with periodic inpatient stays at the hospital for medical procedures. Wolfson had very limited means. His assets were nominal at best (even after a lifetime of saving) and resided in secure and insured bank-issued products such as certificates of deposit and money market funds. He had equity in his home and had an account at one securities firm, StockCross, and prior to that at Wachovia and TD Waterhouse. Wolfson needed to generate a modest amount of income for his monthly expenses and desired to bequeath his assets upon passing to his heirs."

"Thomas Cooper, the broker, befriended Wolfson in the 1980s shortly after he became widowed. (Remember the story of Lillian Wentz from Chapter Two and how her $24 million fortune was put at risk immediately after her husband died.) Cooper and Wolfson developed a special kinship whereby Cooper thought of Wolfson as a father figure and Wolfson associated Cooper as a pseudo-son."

"Sadly, the person whom Wolfson entrusted with his best interests and to ensure that his 'golden years' were golden, abused the trust. After Cooper accepted the role as Wolfson's fiduciary, he recommended an investment strategy intending to benefit his own pecuniary interests that ultimately resulted in financial ruination for Wolfson. Because Wolfson relied heavily on Cooper's investment advice, he had no knowledge that he was victimized and misled."

Lessons & Takeaways

- Elderly people are especially vulnerable to financial fraud. They're often lonely, they often lack a support system, and can often suffer from Alzheimer's or other illnesses that affect their ability to make lucid decisions.
- Financial serial killers target the elderly. They have been known to compile lists of older people with land, homes, insurance policies, and stocks.
- Elder fraud and abuse is a growing problem in this country. With the increasing number of aging baby boomers, this portion of the population will only increase, creating a bigger pool of targets for con men.
- If you have an elderly parent or family member, keep in touch with that person as regularly as possible. Try to keep an eye on his or her financial matters.
- As hard as it may be to accept, the financial serial killer may be a member of your family. Greedy people can target anyone, and they will prey on the people closest to them, even their own relatives.
- As we said before, *It's twelve noon. Do you know who's treating your mother to a free lunch in Florida to talk about investments with spectacular, market-beating "guaranteed" returns?*

INTERLUDE
D

The Investment Industry Speaks

L eading advisers, executives, lawyers, and investigators from the securities business tell our readers what scams could be prevalent right now and how to avoid them.

Carrie Wisniewski thinks investors should be very careful when a broker or adviser tries to sell them a product that claims it's linked to the alternative energy sector. "It's ripe for the picking. It's in the news, it's politically correct. It's like the perfect storm brewing to get people to invest in every crazy idea: wind, solar, biodiesel. One e-mail I got said, 'Your e-mail came up as an A PLUS investor. We are offering you this opportunity to invest in X, Y & Z.' I said to myself, my *e-mail* is an A PLUS investor? What does that have to do with anything?" People are vulnerable to those kinds of solicitations.

Some schemes could involve a pump-and-dump technique using a stock. The way the adviser would approach the investor is how the investment is structured, she says. It could be a private placement, meaning little disclosure to the SEC, or a stock offering or promissory note. "What investors really need to do is get out there and kick the tires and do some due diligence and not just look at the offering document the adviser hands you," she says. "If it's a significant investment, and private placements often have minimums of $50,000 to $100,000, you should get on a plane and go there. Do they really have an office, or is the home address an empty construction trailer? See if it looks like a viable ongoing business, with real people behind it. So many of these things are fabricated around peoples' kitchen tables, and it's all just hot air. Which brings us back to alternative energy," she says with a laugh.

Coauthor Bruce Kelly believes that the World Wide Web poses a number of dangers for investors. The Internet does allow clients 24-hour access to their accounts and the ability to find out information about financial professionals through Google and various databases. That's a clear positive for investors.

But financial serial killers are rapidly becoming more adept at using investors' belief in the sanctity of the Web as part of the con.

Regulators in Britain have warned investors that fraudulent cold callers refer clients to phony Web sites in order to gain their trust. The sites look just as good as a real legitimate investment business, but the Web sites are easily faked.

In fact, boiler room firms were masquerading as reputable broker-dealers, *London's Daily Telegraph* reported. Overseas financial serial killers were using the names, registration numbers, and addresses of authorized, legitimate firms. The financial serial killers were also using "cloned copies of legitimate companies' Web sites, but changing important details such as phone numbers and e-mail addresses," the *Telegraph* said.

Professor Larry Sullivan thinks that Medicare and managed-care fraud could escalate, particularly as new laws and procedures come into effect with the overhaul of the health care insurance system.

"My mother was in a nursing home—in a hospice. These doctors did not even have an office. They had answering services. There were so many elderly people. The doctors would walk in the room and say *hello Veronica how are you doing*? That was a visit. A $150 bill went to the insurance company for that. And, he must have done 200 visits a day. This was all—to the insurance companies—all legal."

Another example of Medicare fraud is when doctors perform unnecessary tests for which they bill the insurance companies, Sullivan says. "You go in and you have an eye exam and all of a sudden they're doing something else to you, too. It's just a little bit here and there."

Jim Rothenberg fears the potential of an orchestrated global crisis—a terrorist act—that could wipe out the stock market and the U.S. capital markets, therefore destroying our country.

"I worked in the New York Stock Exchange. I was chief counsel for market surveillance in 1973 and 1974, during the Cold War." Rothenberg feared that the Soviet Union would create a global crisis to gain control of the stock market, and a contemporary analogy exists today. "The United States imports 15 percent of its oil from Venezuela. Venezuela is doing increasing deals with China. Venezuela announces, after it establishes a long position in oil (therefore betting oil prices will rise)—in oil contracts and oil stocks—that it's not going to sell any more oil to the United States."

"Now if 15 percent of the oil coming into this country is immediately cut off, what is going to happen to oil future contracts?" The contracts will explode in value."

The U.S. capital markets are extraordinarily vulnerable to countries manipulating stocks, he says. "What if Venezuela cut off the oil tomorrow? I've thought about this for thirty-five years. When you're talking about national security, the economic foundation is the securities markets. Someone who can effectively destroy that market is going a long way in destroying the American economic picture. If we don't have a capital market in this country—where you can secondarily trade stock—then you can't issue stock. And companies can't get their hands on capital to increase and build business."

Our own human nature and optimism can do us in when it comes to investing, says Mal Makin, a veteran broker and financial planner. He started his firm, the Professional Planning Group of Westerly, Rhode Island, in 1976, and it now has $364 million in client assets.

Investors' optimism can often prove extremely dangerous, he says. "The danger right now is, as a species, we are way too hopeful and optimistic when it comes to our own good. The frauds that are perpetrated against us are frauds that defy common sense. There's something deep inside us that says, *maybe this really could be the biggest gold discovery ever.*

"The Madoff scam involved a lot of very well-educated people who never asked a question because they didn't want to hear the answer," he says. Clients tricked themselves into believing Madoff was for real, he says. "Since it was happening and working, why pursue it?"

"We are far too trusting, optimistic, and forgetful of things that can hurt us," he says. "That's who we are as people, and that's who we are as a species. For many of us, God made our glass half full, as opposed to half empty. We want the thing to work."

That clearly carries over into investing, Makin says. "We believe the guy who says he can buy the penny stock, take a 30 percent commission, and double our money in six months. We know it can't happen, but people fall for it."

Investors want to trust their brokers and advisers, but that can sometimes cause harm, he says. "There is a certain type of person, probably the majority, who wants to have above all else a clear transparent trusting relationship with the advisers. They say, 'I trust you,' and that's the end of the conversation."

That can prove dangerous. "Some people do that out of laziness. They don't want to ask questions or be involved. Some behave that way out of ignorance. A large group of folks simply want to trust. That is probably the single most dangerous attitude anyone who is buying anything can have, but particularly in the investment field, where it's so complex and has so many moving parts. There's so much paper."

Makin believes in forcing clients to pay attention and ask questions, in order to understand as much as they can. "They have to at least hear it, and if they don't remember, they know that information and an explanation at least exists."

The efficiency of the Internet can pose a danger, Makin says. "Investors can shut off paper and have everything delivered via the Internet. They can shut off certain statements from a brokerage firm. That can make investing cloudier and more difficult to understand."

CHAPTER
SEVENTEEN

Tilting at Windmills: How One Investor Refused to Give Up His Fight to Track Down His Financial Serial Killer

Harris "Butch" Ballow pleaded guilty in 2004 to one of the largest stock fraud cases in Texas history, but before he was sentenced to federal prison, he skipped town. Now the guy who swindled hundreds of people is living the good life in Mexico, Panama, and Costa Rica.

One of Butch's victims was Houston businessman Jakie Sandefer. Jakie is a seventy-three-year-old self-made oil man, having grown up and worked in the rough and tumble oil patch. Like many of his generation, Jakie's word is his bond and he has done many a deal based on a handshake.

Jakie crossed paths with Butch in early 1996 when a friend, a Houston stockbroker, called Jakie about a hot new stock, Titan Resources. "My broker had never tried to sell me anything before," Jakie says. "When a guy you know and who is a friend tells you something, and he is so certain, I didn't even get the details." The Titan stock tanked soon thereafter, and Jakie and his business partner lost their $360,000 investment.

The collapse of Titan Resources attracted the attention of federal regulators. Investigations launched by the SEC, U.S. Attorney's office, as well as lawyers for its investors, exposed a fraud behind the company's curtain. Titan Resource's principal, Butch Ballow, and his associates had created a number of shell companies to buy and sell stock among themselves, which artificially pumped up the stock prices in the process. Butch convinced investors to buy in to the deal for shares of the pumped-up stock. He would then sell *his* shares at the inflated price (in Titan's case, millions) before the bottom fell out—leaving everyone else with worthless stock.

Not only did Jakie and his partner lose their money but so did hundreds of other investors. Court records show that "Butch Ballow . . . directed cash and securities in excess of $100 million through the accounts of his various sham corporations" in just three years.

Butch carried out the Titan fraud while living in an upscale home in the small Texas community of Tiki Island, and while worshiping in his local church. The corporations he controlled donated nearly $500,000 to the Abundant Life Christian Center in La Marque. He actively used his standing in the church to bolster his credibility with investors.

Jakie sued Butch and the brokerage firm and won back the full amount that they had invested in Titan Resources. The jury also awarded them punitive damages of $8 million against the brokerage firm and $4 million against Butch. Jakie had established at trial that Butch generated misleading press releases saying that Titan Resources had completed several major deals for drilling operations, when those deals had actually never been closed. The brokerage firm was found responsible for introducing its customers to Butch while knowing that some of the publicity claims about Titan were false.

For Jakie, victory in the lawsuit against Butch was only a partial win; he still had to collect the money from Butch, who now claimed that he had no money or property.

While Jakie was trying to collect the money he had won in his lawsuit, the elusive Butch Ballow continued to live comfortably in his $700,000 three-story Tiki Island home. He traveled around the country in a private jet owned by one of the corporations that he controlled. Butch's lavish lifestyle was apparently funded exclusively by these sham corporations that were set up in other people's names and that never paid taxes or conducted legitimate business. "He doesn't own a thing, and he lives like a king," Jakie said after the trial. "He's living in a million-dollar house, rides around in two airplanes, has a ranch, and a boat." Jakie hired a private investigator, John Moritz, to find out where and how Butch was hiding assets from collection.

One of the shell companies that Butch used for protection was Recreational Park Properties Inc. Although defunct, it was listed by the appraisal district as being the owner of Butch's Tiki Island home. Butch's brother-in-law was listed as the president of Recreational Park.

Butch had a nice pair of wheels, owned by another sham corporation. Butch's $63,000 Jaguar sedan was registered to Texas Investments Inc., a British Virgin Islands corporation.

But after intense investigative hunting and pressure by Moritz and Jakie's lawyers, Butch finally agreed to work out a deal to pay back Jakie some of the money he had won at trial.

Moritz says that Butch Ballow is the best con man he has ever seen. "Ballow would use the approach of 'well . . . preacher so-and-so knows me well. Go ask him about me.' So he got his reputation through a lot of church groups."

Complaints to the FBI and U.S. Attorney by Jakie and other investors resulted in an FBI investigation into Butch. After several years, Butch was arrested in late 2002. His home was raided by FBI agents who carried away his computer and documents. He was charged with conducting a stock fraud and money-laundering scheme that cost certain brokerage firms nearly $7 million. The U.S. Attorney handling the case said "the fraud alleged in the complaint is just the tip of the iceberg. The damage to individual investors is incalculable."

The U.S. Attorney said that Butch had indeed used sham domestic and offshore corporations to cheat brokers. Butch had named as officers of these corporations his relatives and friends, as well as his secretary, his brother's handyman, and a man who had maintained his yacht. Butch's name never appeared in the corporate records or on the accounts through which he was conducting his fraud.

He used these sham corporations to con brokerage firms into financing stock purchases by his numerous shell companies. The government charged that Butch gave false information to the brokerages about his companies' creditworthiness and then opened accounts to get financing from the brokerages in order to buy stocks. The brokerages held the stocks as collateral while Butch used the loans for his own personal benefit, including his personal purchases and to pay the individuals who he had listed as the company officers.

The government attorneys also charged that Butch had used the corporations to trade stocks between them to give the appearance that there was significant activity involving the stocks, thus raising their value. Butch went to brokerage firms, borrowed money, and offered the inflated shares as collateral for big-dollar loans. But once the stocks' overvaluation was discovered, their prices plummeted. The brokerage firms would call in their loans, since the stock collateral had fallen in value. The sham companies did not have the money to pay back the loans, and the brokerages were left holding worthless stock.

Butch agreed to plead guilty to one count of federal wire fraud charges and was scheduled for sentencing. Before he was sentenced, he offered to cooperate with prosecutors and tell them who else was involved in his various stock swindles. He promised that he would point fingers and explain in detail the full breadth of the scams. In exchange for his cooperation, the government offered that it would recommend that he serve a reduced prison sentence.

Once arrested, Butch was held in jail because he was considered to be a flight risk. He was known to spend time in Mexico and Panama so the government had successfully argued that he be detained.

After he pleaded guilty, but before the date of his sentencing hearing, Butch asked to be released from jail for thirty days so that he could wind up his personal affairs and prepare for his prison term. Even though Butch was considered to be an extreme flight risk, he apparently was able to convince the federal government to let him temporarily leave prison; the government was eager to work this deal since he had promised to give up all the information he had on stock swindles in Texas. And since he had been released once during his trial for a relative's funeral, and returned as promised, the government was lulled into thinking that he would return to turn himself back in to the authorities. So Butch was released until his sentencing hearing, where he faced being locked up in prison for ten years.

This time, however, the overweight, unassuming man with the religious flair fled the country. On the day of sentencing, Butch didn't show up. When he failed to appear, the federal judge criticized both prosecutors and defense attorneys for allowing the known scam artist to disappear. The judge issued an arrest warrant, but remarked that Butch had probably escaped to a beach in Panama, one of the locations where he had business ties.

• --

Financial serial killers know how to slip through the cracks and keep on stealing.

-- •

Jakie was absolutely incensed. How could the government have let this known con artist, an admitted felon, waltz right out of prison? "This guy conned all the investors, and now he conned the federal government," Jakie decried. "It's the silliest thing you ever heard of. This guy was a flight risk from day one."

A Houston attorney who represented Butch in the criminal case says his client initially cooperated with the government, so much so that he personally vouched for the man. This lawyer had told the judge of the case and the government lawyers that his client would temporarily leave the prison to wrap up his affairs, but he would come right back. "I've never done that before. Never ever done that before—and I probably will never do it again given what happened in Ballow's case," the lawyer told a Houston news station.

"It just goes to show you the level of how big a con guy he really is and always was," says Jakie's investigator John Moritz. "They should have recognized that. Shame on them."

Jakie leapt back into action, reached into his own pocket, and decided to fund Moritz to track down Butch. Jakie had collected from Butch the money he lost on the fraudulent stock deal, so he wasn't owed any more cash. But this was about more than money. Butch had swindled hundreds of people, many of whom could not afford to hire a lawyer to sue Butch or track down his assets. Jakie had been fortunate in business and had the financial means to pursue Butch. Most other victims did not have this luxury.

Butch was a thief. A financial serial killer. And that type of person, Jakie believed, had to be stopped. He had to serve his time in prison. Butch had even admitted his guilt in commiting this felony. It wasn't right that this guy could be left to run free on the beaches of Panama and Mexico.

So Moritz was hired back on the case. He has stayed on Butch's trail for over four years, and has located him at five sunny locations: Panama, Costa Rica, and in Mérida, Cancún, and Puerto Aventura, Mexico. Moritz has photographed Butch inside a gated waterfront community in Mexico, along with his condo, his restaurant, and his two yachts.

The financial serial killer can never stop. Moritz says that Butch is running new stock investment scams from his hideouts in Central and South America. Butch's new scheme is to form companies, set up Web sites, and raise money via the Internet. One of his companies is Calypso Wireless in Panama. Another, Red Dog, claims to plan the import of amphibious vehicles from China. In Cancún, Butch is running a luxury golf course development called Monarch Cancún. "I actually went down and took a look at this one, and it wasn't anything but bare-ass ground," recalls Moritz.

Moritz says he's frustrated because every time he's located Butch, he handed over all his information to both the FBI and the U.S. Marshal Service. Neither authority has bothered to pursue Ballow, and he remains a free man.

Life on the lam is not affecting Butch Ballow in any way. "It's not wearing on him. He's living the good life. He thinks he's invincible," says Moritz. And so far, he is. Despite the fact that Moritz knows exactly where Butch is living, and has collected a trove of evidence about him, the U.S. authorities have yet to nab Butch and bring him back to serve his prison term.

The Houston lawyer who represented Butch, and vouched that he would not flee, says, "I'm stunned, given the investigation that Moritz has done, that he's not been picked up by the authorities."

When a Houston television station tried to speak with the attorney who defended Butch in Jakie's lawsuit, the lawyer declined the station's request for an interview, but did say, "If you talk to Butch, tell him he still owes me $75,000." Obviously, this lawyer didn't know that he was representing a financial serial killer. If he had been able to identify this type of con man, he wouldn't have been scammed too.

CHAPTER
EIGHTEEN

The Psychology Behind
Why We Fall for Scams

There are many reasons why we fall for investment scams or make investment mistakes. We have to appreciate that we are human and our psychology can lead us to make the wrong investment decisions. As we understand and realize these factors, we are less likely to fall prey to the financial serial killer.

Dr. Robert Cialdini was Regents' Professor of Psychology and Marketing at Arizona State University. He has received the Scientific Achievement Award of the Society for Consumer Psychology, the Donald T. Campbell Award for Distinguished Contributions to Social Psychology, and the Peitho Award for Distinguished Contributions to the Science of Social Influence.

Cialdini says that the root cause of people falling victim to a financial fraud is their uncertainty about the details of the financial environment. When people feel uncertain about any decision, including financial ones, they frequently fail to look *to themselves* for answers as to what they should do, because they lack so much confidence and feel so uncertain. So they look outside themselves, and this sets them up for the fraud.

There are two classic places people can look for reassurance that will allow them to reduce their uncertainty. One is to those people who appear to be experts, or at least to those people who proclaim to be experts. Those individuals who have background and experience and credentials in the area. They will defer to those so-called experts under the circumstances. "Those individuals who can present themselves well as experts—who can provide the patina of authority and expertise—will get people to respond automatically to their recommendations and to defer to them," Cialdini remarks.

"There was an interesting study that was done in Texas. Researchers took a man and had him cross the street several times against the light to see how many people would follow behind him. If he was wearing a suit and tie, 350 percent more people followed him into traffic against the light, which was against the law. They followed him because his appearance gave him a sense of authority and made him appear to be a type of an expert. This demonstrates that people will look outside of themselves to the legitimately constituted authorities."

Besides a suit, or maybe a fancy office in a tall skyscraper, there are other symbols of authority that signify an "expert." Things like certifications and diplomas. These kinds of trappings can be sometimes genuine, but are sometimes easily counterfeited to convince people that the holder of these items is somebody who knows what he or she is talking about.

Cialdini explains that "even in Madoff's case, he sat on a governing commission that was designed to offer policing policies for the financial industry. So, he had the second component of what constitutes a great authority in the minds of an audience.

The first is expertise and the second is trustworthiness. Here is a guy who makes it appear that he is concerned about the ethical and proper way to deliver financial information. He sat on the committee that was designed to do that within the NASDAQ. All the while he was gaming the system."

The second place we look when we are uncertain is to people just like us. To our peers, to our contemporaries. "That's why so often these scams turn out to be affinity scams," says Cialdini. "Groups that share some kind of connection, some kind of affiliation. It can be a religious one. It can be an ethnic one. Charles Ponzi exploited other Italian American immigrants. We see cases where Baptists are being scammed by other Baptists. Mormons being scammed by other Mormons. Armenian-Americans being scammed by Armenian-Americans. People use these as a source of good information. 'What are the people like me doing and telling me to do? I can usually trust that.'"

Another compelling psychological factor that leads us to make an investment decision is the perceived scarcity of the investment opportunity. We want to jump into those situations where it appears that there is a restricted opportunity, or a dwindling opportunity, to get involved. "We are drawn to those opportunities that only a few are going to be allowed in, or you have to have a certain level of finances in order to be allowed in, or you have to know somebody to be allowed in. Madoff did that in spades and he had people clamoring to give him their money," explains Cialdini.

Exclusive opportunities, or limited-time offers, are always enticing. "Access to one of these opportunities if it's rare or scarce or dwindling in availability—it makes people a little crazy.

It unhinges their willingness to step back from the situation and think about it because they are being directed by emotional signals inside them rather than cognitive, fully considered approaches," Cialdini cautions.

These psychological impulses come from a number of human needs. We want to feel special. We want to be thought of as one-of-a-kind. We want exclusivity. Cialdini seconds this: "It is typically the case that those things that are rare, those things that are not widely available to people, are more valuable to people. That's why gold is valuable. That's why diamonds are valuable. That's why the purveyors, the miners of gold and diamonds, hold back these items from the market, because the less available they are the more attractive they become." The secretive, or exclusive, factor plays into our psychological need to feel special.

"People like the idea of being unique, being special, being different. Especially if that means that they are afforded certain benefits that others can't get. You can understand why that would be a very attractive proposition."

The irony with Madoff is that all the while he was giving the appearance of running an exclusive operation, he actually represented thousands of people, but he made everyone who was his customer feel like he or she was part of a very exclusive club. In this way, Madoff managed expertly this *illusion* of exclusivity. In this way he mastered the deception.

Madoff may have wanted to be more public about his fund and his supposed investment prowess. He might have even wanted to advertise. However, to the extent that he became more public about his investments and what he was supposedly accomplishing, he would have drawn more attention to his investment returns, which in turn would have likely drawn scrutiny. Someone would have more quickly realized that Madoff was not really bringing in these remarkable returns year after year, month after month.

Madoff's tack, and that of other fraudsters, was to keep his investment formula secret. He made his fund appear very restricted. Cialdini observes that "if anybody challenged him, he threatened to kick them out. So you weren't allowed to really think through all of the issues without potentially losing your ability to be one of the select few in his club."

These psychological needs go beyond the need to feel special or to feel a certain level of status. Cialdini explains this as "the need to be relatively advantaged in terms of resources. So it's not enough just to be doing well, we like the idea of doing better than our neighbors."

We want to feel like we have more than others have. There are two ways to get there: either we move up, or other people move down. Thus the reason why we gloat when others fail. "So you find people taking some kind of joy in seeing those around them fail," says Cialdini. "If they have failed, they like those around them to fail even more. And so it allows them the prestige of being less of a fool than everyone else."

People, including investors, also want consensus. They will follow the lead of those around them. Especially if the leaders appear authoritative, are similar to us, and make us feel special. When we feel like part of a group, then we are more likely to blindly follow.

Financial serial killers are skilled at establishing a connection with their victims. That will be either a pre-existing connection or a newly created connection. Cialdini explains, "The other thing is, of course, the idea of having an existing connection or friendship with the individual who is promoting the scam or some kind of association with people involved in it. Again, if we think about the Madoff case, he had emissaries of various sorts in various religious groups—Jewish congregations—but also in golf clubs. He had people who were selling access to his funds to the people they were friends with within those organizations. That's another thing that we have a weakness for. We tend to be willing to say yes to our friends, because we think they're steering us right, number one. But number two, it's very awkward to say no to a friend who comes to us with a great proposition, and who is staking his or her reputation and status on it. It's difficult to turn down a friend. So that's another aspect that is often part of these scams."

Often we decide to do business with our friends, or someone we know, as opposed to standing back and objectively looking at qualifications. We might have a friend who says he can manage our money, but if we really study his résumé we will come to realize that he is not the most qualified person. Then assume a stranger comes to us with a very qualified résumé and background, and he's proven that he can successfully manage money and has a track record of proven returns. Yet if we don't *know* him we are less likely to let him handle our money.

Cialdini says that this behavior derives from "the belief that we know about the trustworthiness of our friends more than we know about the trustworthiness of a stranger. So when we have a friend we think 'all right, I know this person, he or she knows me, I can trust the advice I get, because this isn't somebody who would consciously try to exploit me.'"

We must conclude here that an investor needs to be careful when doing business with people he or she knows. Keep in mind that your opinion of the person's ability to handle your money will be colored by your relationship with that person.

It's a better method to select a money manager by interviewing two or three candidates and narrowing the choice from there. Some studies conclude that we actually make our decisions based on our emotions and then rationalize them later. Cialdini says that we often do this "but sometimes our brains can actually cause us to evaluate the emotion—not just rationalize it—but catch ourselves. If we truly take a step back and try to be dispassionate about a decision because it's going to involve considerable resources, we can do a pretty good job of countering a purely emotional decision."

In making our investment decisions we need to avoid being gullible and follow a sensible approach to evaluating our choices. There are steps that we can take. Cialdini defines gullibility as "not just an action in a particular situation that turned out to be wrong, but a tendency across all situations in which a person finds him or herself to go along with the appeals or the persuasive communications with others without thinking through the merits of what that person is offering." In other words, being led by the fraudster and not objectively evaluating what he or she is saying to us.

Smart and cautious people can be snared in frauds. This happens often. The financial serial killer plays on our emotions and knows our human frailties. Cialdini knows this can happen to the most cautious of us: "I think that a lot of people who are not traditionally or normally gullible can get caught up in these scams, because it has to do with the distortion of—the undermining of—normally good decision-making principles that people apply. Those normal decisions get twisted in particular situations where they don't really apply. So most of the time, it makes sense to follow the lead of a genuine authority. But sometimes it doesn't because that authority has counterfeited the evidence. Most of the time, it makes sense to follow the lead of what many others like us have done, but sometimes it doesn't because many of those others have been tricked into moving in that direction. Most of the time, it makes sense to seize rare or dwindling opportunities for valuable resources, but some of the time it doesn't because those things have been manufactured or fabricated as rare or dwindling. They are not genuinely rare in the environment. So these normally good decision-making rules can be perverted by con artists and scam artists into tricks."

You first need to understand yourself and the human needs that can make you vulnerable to a fraud. Then you need to objectively evaluate the person who is coming to you and asking to handle your money. Cialdini warns that you need to avoid those people who try to push you into making a decision quickly. Steer clear of those who don't want you to look at or consider other options. Another warning sign is people who are unwilling to give you their background and credentials in ways that allow you to check their expertise in a particular arena. Be suspicious of people who are telling you that you have to act now, otherwise you will not be eligible or you will lose the opportunity.

Investors are even more vulnerable now following the credit crisis, the plunge in the stock market, and the decreased value of their 401(k) and other retirement plans. Everyone has been touched in one way or another by the financial problems of the last several years. The problems with the banks and the financial system are on the front page of the newspaper just about daily.

At first, the normal response to these financial calamities is to be cautious. Sometimes we just freeze. We take no action. At some point, as we emerge from our financial coma, we are faced with the reality of all the money we have lost. At some point many of us will be vulnerable to those magical financial wizards who proclaim that they can rapidly earn back all of our losses.

Cialdini says that there's a particular kind of influence—a certain type of sales pitch—that is likely to be employed, and he's already seen it. "It's likely to be working in the future as well, that will try to move people off the fence and try to get them away from their cautious stand."

Here is how the pitch goes: *This is the time, now is the time, to make your move. Prices have gone down too low. They've bottomed out. They can only go up. You want to get in on the ground floor right now.*

We are already seeing this tack in real estate. Prices have fallen 20 percent or 30 percent. So the experts tell us they can't fall any further. In some parts of the country that is probably true, and it may be time to buy, but in other parts of the country they have yet to hit bottom. We are not saying that prices never bottom out; of course they do. And then they head north. What we are saying is that you must be aware of this type of selling scheme that rushes you into making a financial decision based on the emotional appeal of "hurry, hurry, hurry."

Cialdini says that "it's the scarcity principle that will move people off the fence. When people are dealing with the recent experiences where they've not done well, they don't want to lose any more. So you can tell them that unless they move, they're going to lose the opportunity. It's going to be a lever to get them off the fence. So that's what I'm going to predict—you're going to see a lot of con artists, a lot of scam artists, using that scarcity lever."

They like to tell us: "You need to move quickly now, because the opportunity is going to be gone. You're never going to see low prices like this again, so hurry up and act now. This is a once-in-a-lifetime opportunity!"

In the context of stocks and bonds, you will find this sales pitch from the fraudster whenever the price of the financial instrument has dropped. At this point it can easily be said that the price used to be way up here, and now it's down here. Now it will reverse its course to the South Pole and head back North. Perhaps there's an argument that the company is poised to turn around, or there are signs that the economy is going to get better. In any event, the selling language will revolve around the urgency that "unless you move now, you're going to miss this opportunity."

So perhaps the great irony is that once you have lost money, you become even more vulnerable to losing money again. Once you have your first loss, or are scammed for the first time, you will eventually get to a psychological state of mind where you want to make up your losses. Anyone who can offer you the chance to recover those losses quickly will likely get your attention. So be aware: you are even more vulnerable to fraud after you have lost money.

Cialdini has experienced this firsthand: "I'm working with AARP in phone scams that they've been investigating. A lot of scammers try to operate on the elderly various types of scams where they can get in and buy gold or they can buy property. The elderly person gets burned and they are so ashamed of it that they become vulnerable to the next scam so that they can recoup their losses. They don't want to think of themselves as losers, and they don't want their family to think of them as fools and idiots financially. So they wind up getting in again and losing yet another chunk of their savings."

Certain types of investors have their self-esteem wrapped up in their financial status. These people may find themselves more vulnerable to the next scam because they need to act quickly before their family or friends learn that they've lost their money. They want to recoup their losses and show themselves and those around them that they are not dupes after all.

You need to recognize if you are one of these people. This requires some serious honesty about who you are in relation to your money, and how your perception of and ideas about money affect your understanding of yourself.

Lessons & Takeaways

- A financial serial killer is going to warm us up, and get to our heart and wallet, by making us feel special, unique, and different. Beware of this technique, which is intended to manipulate our emotions.
- We will naturally trust people who we perceive to be just like us. Keep in mind that simply because someone is from our neighborhood or hometown, or shares our same ethnic background, does not mean that the person necessarily has our best interests in mind.
- Simply because your children attend the same school as your broker's children, or you attend the same church or synagogue as him, does not mean that he is qualified to manage your money. Look objectively at his qualifications.
- Beware of the human need for status, and don't get involved in a financial investment solely because it makes you feel important or as though you are part of some type of elite group.
- Just because everyone else is in an investment does not mean that the investment is right for you. Think for yourself, and don't play "follow the leader." That game is for children.
- When choosing a money manager, interview two or three different candidates. Take emotion out of the decision and make an informed decision about who has the best qualifications and track record.
- Remember that once you have lost money, you are more vulnerable to losing money again. When people lose money, they want to hurry up and win it back. That makes them vulnerable to get-rich-quick scams. That emotional urge will also lead to bad investment decisions.

Epilogue

re we a nation filled with Ponzi schemers, rip-off artists, and get-rich-quick dreamers? Of course we are. There are many in our country who want to make easy money; they dream of fast riches, a mansion on the beach, and laying in the sun. They want to do it with your money.

Financial serial killers are dangerous for two reasons. First, they epitomize the shallowness of the get-rich-quick schemes. Like any criminal, they don't want to work for money but desire the trappings of success. Second, and more importantly to you, the financial serial killer will hone in on your dreams of wealth and financial security for your family, exploit them, and destroy them.

The current economic environment is fertile ground for financial serial killers. Not only are we a nation of dreamers, more of us are desperate to hang on to what we have. Are the poor and the middle class being squeezed? Of course they are. Middle-class income is stagnant. Unemployment has hit record highs. Meanwhile, the costs of a college education and health care are out of control. Financial serial killers promise to relieve us of our financial desperation. Instead, of course, they make it much, much worse.

It's obvious that investors need greater protection. Remember, we live in an age when the number of people receiving a guaranteed pension from an employer is dwindling. Everyone is left to fend for themselves financially, even as we all live longer.

What does this all mean? First and foremost, you must attempt to guard your financial safety. Your financial adviser or stockbroker has to tell you *how* he's working for you. If he can't, you should seriously reconsider the relationship.

The zeal of Wall Street lobbyists to stop efforts by Congress to shape meaningful financial reforms knows no bounds. Wall Street and the rest of the financial services industry has incredible wealth at its disposal, and therefore has incredible muscle.

A recent article from *Bloomberg BusinessWeek* showed the size of that muscle.

Congress is attempting to push the securities industry and its 634,000 salespeople to work as fiduciaries. Wall Street, of course, hates the idea, because it would mean their brokers would be held to a much higher level of accountability then they are now. That could bog down sales and lead to higher costs defending against investor lawsuits.

Many brokers already adhere to a fiduciary standard, but it's their choice to do so. The mind-set of the typical broker, however, is that of a salesperson. Selling products and acting as a fiduciary do not go hand in hand. "Lobbying by insurers and banks including Morgan Stanley may result in the elimination of a proposed new standard that would make retail brokers more accountable to clients," the article said.

Of course, consumers want more protection from Congress, not the same old thing.

"Retail investors have suffered incredible losses in the recent crisis," Barbara Roper, director of investor protection for the Consumer Federation of America, told *BusinessWeek*. "This provision would at least help protect investors against some of the toxic investments they were peddled by their financial advisers."

There will always be crime in society. Muggings on the street, thefts, and murders. That's why we have police and laws. There will always be financial crime and scams. That's why we have financial regulators and laws, to stop those types of financial crimes.

Our police and our regulators can fail us. They can't catch all the criminals, so we need to look out for ourselves, too. There is no excuse for financial fraud. Once you understand the mind of the financial serial killer you will be better equipped to take steps to protect yourself, your family, and your friends from the pernicious attacks being mounted everyday by con men and scam artists who are intent on breaking the law and stealing our hard-earned savings.

Wall Street is always developing new financial products to sell you. The ability of these guys to develop new products moves at a quick pace. It is a challenge for the regulators, like the SEC, to keep up with these new products, to understand them, and to regulate them. We would estimate that it takes the regulators at least three or four years (and in many cases longer) to catch up to Wall Street in understanding products that they are selling to investors.

Wall Street and human nature are inexorably linked. Jesse Livermore was a famous early twentieth-century trader and speculator who was immortalized in the 1923 book *Reminiscences of a Stock Operator* by Edwin Lefevre. Many consider Livermore one of the greatest traders and speculators who ever lived. He spent his life on Wall Street, and this is how he summed it all up:

> "Wall Street never changes, the pockets change, the suckers change, the stocks change, but Wall Street never changes, because human nature never changes."

There's a financial serial killer in your town. Now, if you meet him, you can spot him, and if you feel like it, tell him to go to hell. We wish you good luck. Protect your wealth, be it large or small. Prosperous and safe investing.

Tom Ajamie and Bruce Kelly,
August 2010

A Laundry List of the Classic Warning Signs for Investors

White-collar crime can and does pay, and it pays because of you. You can prevent that. We present a concise guide to spotting fraud and avoiding the loss of your life savings to a scam artist, whether it's $10,000 or $10,000,000.

- Is the broker or adviser using high-pressure sales tactics and telling you that this investment is a great offer and you have to invest right now?
- Is the broker or adviser pursuing your business and pressuring you just as you are dealing with a dramatic life change like the death of a loved one, particularly a spouse who handled the money?
- Is the broker or adviser telling you the investment has a guaranteed return of 10 percent, 15 percent, or higher? Does he repeatedly tell you that the return is guaranteed, and there is no risk to your investment?
- Does the broker or adviser hold his clients' assets with a firm or outside custodian whose name you know and whose history you can research easily online?

- Can you find out information about the broker or adviser and his firm at public Web sites such as www.FINRA.org, www.cfp.net, or www.sec.gov? If you can't find public information about the broker or adviser, you should be highly wary and probably stay away.
- Does the broker or adviser simply not explain his investments or strategies, saying they are too complex or of a top-secret proprietary nature that no one but he can understand?
- Does he spend money in a lavish and extravagant manner, with homes and cars that don't match the level of income you believe he is making?
- Are you desperate for money? Or are you greedy? Is your broker or adviser pushing your greed button?
- What is your family treasure? It's probably not a $24 million pot of gold like Lillian Wentz's, but it still has incredible value. Do you understand how to pass your estate, be it a piece of property, a chunk of stock, or your retirement account, to the next generation?
- Older women can be particularly vulnerable to such scams in times of grief.
- Money can bring out the worst in people. Be careful. Even family members can turn against family members.
- People are very vulnerable after the death of loved ones, be they spouses, children, parents, lovers, or friends. Be careful of making any immediate decisions, particularly if the professional giving advice is pressuring you to make a decision.
- Con artists can be reputable members or pillars of the community. When it comes to your money, carefully question to whom you give it.

- When investing, avoid bubbles, hype, and hysteria.
- There is no new paradigm.
- No market trend, up or down, lasts forever.
- The investment guru who has a secret method of making riches could well be a flimflam man.
- Is your investment adviser too perfect? Like Madoff, is he or she generating returns that, year in, year out, closely resemble each other?
- There's a tremendous amount of work that goes into hyping a stock or something precious like gold. If you can learn to detect the hype, you can protect your savings from the financial serial killers who could be targeting you.
- Investors need to be careful of promotion and hype through investment newsletters. Who knows if they are independent? Money could be exchanging hands to determine if a company is going to be included in these newsletters. Or, the newsletter writers could simply be buddies of the executives running the companies they claim to be covering without a bias. They hold themselves out as independent newsletters providing exclusive, insider knowledge—and charge a steep price—but many question their independence. There is really no monitoring of those newsletters, and there really are hundreds of them, with many focusing on risky areas such as oil and gas and other commodities.
- Winning over the media is important to give the appearance of legitimacy to a fraud. With the reach of the Internet and 24-hour business news coverage in television, there are more ways than ever for a fraud to reach into your home.
- Journalists earn their pay and reputation for "breaking news," for reporting stories and information before the

competition. Even the most talented and conscientious reporter may get facts wrong and make mistakes. In other words, just because a reporter wrote a story about a company or financial transaction does not mean it is correct.

- Great investment opportunities are often kept secret. By the time the average person hears about a wonderful opportunity, the easy money has probably already been made. Real opportunities or real ways to make money are treated like state secrets. In the case of Bre-X, the executives with the company took a worthless patch of land and used it to create a stock that was worth billions.

- Just because a broker works for a large, national firm, with thousands of brokers occupying expensive offices, is no insurance that your broker is not a financial serial killer. Because Enrique Perusquia worked for Paine Webber, he appeared to be reputable on the surface. Simply put, there is not as much protection as you would think.

- Sometimes, a screening or compliance process can break down, and sometimes it happens with the firm's biggest, most important advisers. That can lead to investors having a false sense of security. Perusquia received kickback checks sent to the office and no one caught on to him. He transferred money to his own account from the customer's account at the brokerage firm, and no one caught on.

- Who's gaining from the transaction you are about to enter into? Is it you or some financial institution?

- Have you asked how the transaction works? Exactly how much are you paying here? Does the answer make sense?

- Beware of commodities and leverage, or borrowing to pay for securities transactions.

- Securities firms are not allowed to use the word "guarantee" in reference to stocks.
- Keep calm. The market is going to be open every day. Know who you are. So, when someone calls you and says, *If you don't do this right now, you're going to miss it*, be willing to miss it.
- Slow down. If you find a broker or adviser, look them up on the Internet (see Chapter Fourteen) before investing.
- Remember the broker is part of a wider corporate culture. If he's not selling product, management simply could stop saying *hello* to him.
- Beware of the "life settlements" market, in which investors buy life insurance policies and collect the policy when the original policyholder dies. There's something unsavory about investing in how long someone will live.
- The investor can't be lazy. Is making eight percent and not understanding how it's done worth more than making four percent and understanding the process?
- Stratton Oakmont and Duke—the names sound more like country clubs than real businesses. Be wary of firms out there that want to appear to be something that they are not. Ask about the name. Can I speak to Mr. Stratton or Mr. Oakmont? Is there really a Mr. Duke somewhere?
- If you invest in high-risk hedge funds or private placements, are you prepared to lose every cent you invested in that fund or offering? If not, don't do it.
- Although they are trying to take a more aggressive stance and proactive steps against fraud, securities regulators have a history of being slow to become involved in cases and, as

Bernie Madoff and Allen Stanford showed, appear out of their league when confronting industry big shots.

- Don't let names and titles confuse you when you seek to work with a financial professional. Ask him how he is registered, with FINRA or the SEC. If he is not registered, and you can't find a history of him or his firm online with regulators, be extremely careful about giving this person your money.

- Never make an investment transaction that hinges upon selling your home or taking out a mortgage on your home. This is a proven recipe for disaster.

- Be skeptical of any investment opportunity that is not in writing. Fraudsters often avoid putting things in writing, but legitimate investments are usually in writing. Avoid an investment if you are told by someone that they do "not have the time to reduce to writing" the particulars about the investment. You should also be suspicious if you are told to keep the investment opportunity confidential.

- Fraudsters are increasingly using the Internet to target particular groups through e-mail spam, the SEC warns. If you receive an unsolicited e-mail from someone you don't know, containing a "can't-miss" investment, your best move is to pass up the "opportunity."

Notes

Chapter 1:

InvestmentNews, "Number of busted Ponzi schemes more than tripled in 2009," December 28, 2009.

Reading Eagle, "Customers surprised good deals went sour: Many say they face larger mortgage principals, higher interest rates, bigger payments and the loss of thousands of dollars," September 21, 2007.

Salt Lake Tribune, "Leaders caution faithful on scams," March 14, 2008.

Chapter 3:

Interview with Professor Larry Sullivan, November 2009.

New York Post, "Sky 'Houdini' Is Grounded," January 14, 2009.

New York Times, "Lost Manuscript Unmasks Details of Original Ponzi," May 5, 2009.

New Yorker, "Madoff and His Models," March 23, 2009.

Chapter 4:

BusinessWeek, "After Bre-X, the Glow is Gone," April 14, 2007.

Fortune, "It Makes Me Sick Every Time I Think About It," June 9, 1997.

Newsweek, "Visions of El Dorado," April 7, 1997.

Fool's Gold: The Making of a Global Market Fraud, Knopf Canada, 1998.

Interlude A:

Interview with Larry Papike, November 2009.

Chapter 5:

BusinessWeek, "A Star Broker's Trail of Losses," June 5, 2000.

U.S. Securities and Exchange Commission, administrative proceeding, "In the matter of Enrique E. Perusquia," November 20, 2002.

Chapter 6:

Interview with David K., ex–Stratton Oakmont broker, August 2009.

Jordan Belfort, *The Wolf of Wall Street*, October 2007.

Associated Press, "US fund manager sentenced in fraud scheme," January 12, 2010.

Chapter 7:

New York Times, "14 Charged with Insider Trading in Galleon Case," November 6, 2009.

New York Times, "Did Galleon Fall Through the Cracks Before?" December 7, 2009.

BusinessWeek, "The SEC's Tough New Offensive on Insider Trading," October 21, 2009.

New York Times, "Hints of Missed Chance to Pursue Galleon Case," October 30, 2009.

Wall Street Journal, "The Man Who Wired Silicon Valley," December 29, 2009.

InvestmentNews, "Risks of Reg D deals worry state regulators," September 27, 2009.

InvestmentNews, "State regulator says SEC dropped the ball on private placements," January 14, 2009.

Commonwealth of Massachusetts, Office of the Secretary of the Commonwealth, Securities Division, Administrative Complaint, In the Matter of Securities America, January 26, 2010.

InvestmentNews, "Execs must answer tough questions at Securities America," January 31, 2010.

Chapter 8:

Bloomberg.com, "Madoff 'Astonished' SEC failed to Act After Interview," September 3, 2009.

Washington Post, "The Madoff Files: A Chronicle of SEC Failure," September 3, 2009.

New York Times, "Report Details How Madoff's Web Ensnared S.E.C.," September 3, 2009.

CNNMoney.com, "Madoff whistleblower blasts SEC," February 4, 2009.

United States Securities and Exchange Commission, Office of Investigations, "Investigation of Failure of the SEC to Uncover Bernard Madoff's Ponzi Scheme," August 31, 2009.

InvestmentNews, "Ex-exec at Stratton Oakmont guilty of fraud—again," November 25, 2009.

The Washington Post, "SEC suspected R. Allen Stanford of Ponzi scheme 12 years earlier, report says," April 17, 2010.

The Wall Street Journal, "Report says regulator missed shots at Stanford," April 17–18, 2010.

InvestmentNews, "With FINRA in red, officials saw green," December 6, 2009.

InvestmentNews, "FINRA must review its exam process for broker-dealers," October 11, 2009.

Interlude B:

Interview with Terry Lister, February 2010.

Interview with Carrie Wisniewski, December 2009.

Chapter 9:

New York Times, "Struggling Over a Rule For Brokers," February 16, 2010.

Ken Fisher, with Lara Hoffman, *How To Smell A Rat: The Five Signs of Financial Fraud,* John Wiley & Sons Inc., 2009.

Chapter 10:

New York Times, "Panel Told of F.B.I. Efforts to Fight Financial Crime," January 15, 2010.

Miami Herald, "Ex-convicts active in mortgage fraud," July 20, 2008.

Interview with Jake Zamansky, October 2009.

Zamansky, www.zamansky.com, "Mortgage Fraud: East Coast, West Coast and Everywhere in Between," July 9, 2007.

Chapter 11:

Interview with John Moscow, February 2010.

Interview with Jake Zamansky, October 2009.

Bloomberg, "Stanford prayer with dying man pumped agents in Alleged Fraud," March 2, 2009.

Interlude C:

Interview with Paul Comstock, January 2010.

Chapter 12:

Wall Street Journal, "SEC Floats Proposals to Open Up 'Dark Pools,'" October 22, 2009.

Morningstar Inc. data.

John Bogle, Blair Academy Reception, New York, N.Y., October 14, 2008.

Interview with Jim Rothenberg, October 2009.

Gary Weiss, *Wall Street Versus America: The Rampant Greed and Dishonesty that Imperil Your Investments*, The Penguin Group, 2006.

Chapter 14:

Washington Post, "Resources for background on your broker," November 15, 2009.

Kiplinger, "How to Spot Trouble With a Financial Adviser," October 2009.

Chapter 15:

InvestmentNews, "Pressure mounts to remove banned Cincinnati broker from elected office," January 15, 2010.

InvestmentNews, "Adviser who calls himself 'child of God' sentenced to 40 months in jail," September 3, 2009.

InvestmentNews, "Ex-AIG adviser who practiced voodoo on victims gets 12 years for fraud," September 13, 2009.

InvestmentNews, "A soldier's story: Wounded vet says Wachovia took away his customers," December 20, 2009.

Chapter 16:

National Center on Elder Abuse, www.ncea.aoa.gov.

InvestmentNews, "Brokerage hit with triple damages in 95-year-old's arbitration award," January 10, 2010.

Motion for Punitive Damages, David Wolfson Living Trust vs. Stockcross Financial Services Inc., et al., November 10, 2009.

Office of Compliance Inspections and Examinatins, Securities and Exchanger Commission, "Protecting Senior Investors: Report of Examinations of Securities Firms providing free lunch sales seminars," September 2007.

Interlude D:

Daily Telegraph, "Boiler rooms turn up the heat on investors," February 26, 2010.

Interview with Mal Makin, March 2010.

Chapter 17:

Houston Chronicle, "Judge OKs $12 million verdict against brokerage firm, PR chief," August 10, 1999.

Houston Chronicle, "Victims help expose swindler's web of schemes," July 29, 2001.

Houston Chronicle, "Past investors lament failed deals of a lifetime," July 29, 2001.

Houston Chronicle, "Lawsuit seeks $456,000 donated to church," September 8, 2001.

Houston Chronicle, "FBI holds man in stock scheme," November 28, 2002.

Houston Chronicle, "Losses in stock scam called incalculable," November 30, 2002.

Houston Chronicle, "Convicted con man absent at sentencing," December 17, 2004.

Houston Chronicle, "FBI seeks help in search for con man," April 21, 2008.

Interview with Jakie Sandefer, January 2010.

Interview with John Mortiz, March 2010.

Chapter 18:

Interview with Dr. Robert Cialdini, January 2010.

Epilogue:

New York Times, "Lobbyists Mass to Try to Shape Financial Reform," October 14, 2009.

Bloomberg BusinessWeek, "Lobbying May Kill Fiduciary-Rules Plan for Brokers," February 12, 2010.

Acknowledgments

Tom Ajamie

I would like to express my sincere appreciation to my friend and coauthor Bruce Kelly. There is no finer financial reporter in the country, and Bruce's contribution to his field and to investors everywhere will be appreciated for many years.

I am also grateful to Tiffany for her encouragement and patience with my work schedule.

Finally, I am eternally indebted to my parents Ed and Elaine for the sacrifices that they made for their children, especially in raising us in a supportive household and assuring us a good education.

Bruce Kelly

It's astounding the number of people who are instrumental in getting a book done, particularly a first book from a team of authors.

First, I would like to thank Kathryn Lineberger, who listened to my many stories of sleazy brokers and fraud beginning in 2007, well before Bernie Madoff confessed to his crimes. She also watched over our son and daughter, Orlando and Vivienne, while I stole away for many hours to work on the book over the weekends.

I would like to thank my dad and brother Tom for their constant love and support over the years. I owe each of my cousins, Christa, Alex, and Alicia, and aunts and uncle, Arden, Priscilla, and Tim, thanks for their constant support and good cheer.

A number of families other than my own have given me great encouragement over the years, including the Nash, Jenkins, and Caplan clans. Thank you. Thanks to the guys at the Dublin House, who listened to stories of financial shenanigans and screw-ups for the last decade.

To the finest reporting buddies a guy could have: Jeff Nash, Matt Quinn, Andrew Osterland, Damian Fowler, and Mark Bruno. I owe each of you my gratitude, and a few rounds, too.

To colleagues at Crain Communications Inc. and *InvestmentNews*, particularly my editor, Jim Pavia, and publisher, Suzanne Siracuse, I owe deep thanks. Jim and Suzanne supported my work on this project 100 percent, and a reporter facing deadlines each day can't ask more than that.

Tom and I would like to thank, once again, everyone we interviewed for the book and was so generous with their time: Professor Larry Sullivan, Tom Barden, Jake Zamansky, Amber Eichner, David K., Larry Papike, Terry Lister, Carrie Wisniewski, Jim Rothenberg, John Moscow, Paul Comstock, Dr. Robert Cialdini, Thomas Willcuts, Jakie Sandefer, and Mal Makin. Thanks to Chistopher J. Carroll for his editorial guidance. Tom's staff at Ajamie LLP, especially Debbie Molloy, gave immeasurable help and assistance.

Tom and I had the good fortune to find our agent, Cynthia Manson, who was immediately excited about the project. She then placed it in front of Herman Graf, a peerless editor at Skyhorse Publishing. Thank you both for your energy, effort, and patience with the project.

Finally, I would like to thank my friend and coauthor, Tom Ajamie. This book was a true collaboration, and working with Tom and chronicling his outrageous stories about the investment business is a true highlight of my career. Tom, what are we going to write about next?